Flashes of the Present Pain

(POETRY QUARTETS)

Sabah Michael Yacoub

WESTBOW
PRESS®
A DIVISION OF THOMAS NELSON
& ZONDERVAN

WestBow Press books may be ordered through booksellers or by contacting:

WestBow Press
A Division of Thomas Nelson & Zondervan
1663 Liberty Drive
Bloomington, IN 47403
www.westbowpress.com
1 (866) 928-1240

ISBN: 978-1-9736-7356-9 (sc)
ISBN: 978-1-9736-7358-3 (hc)
ISBN: 978-1-9736-7357-6 (e)

Library of Congress Control Number: 2019912853

Print information available on the last page.

WestBow Press rev. date: 9/05/2019

وَمَضاتُ الألمِ الحاضرْ
"رباعيات شعرية"

صباح ميخائيل يعقوب

1

Dedication

To the spirit of my father who taught me that stumbling is a forward jump.

To the spirit of my mother who flooded me with fondness that filled my entire life with love.

To the spirit of my elder brother whose sudden departure left me in despair.

To my wife who adorned my thoughts with her fruitful encouragement and active support.

To my two daughters and my son who added to the family house happiness and charm.

To those who have learned a lesson from the hardships of their time.

ألإهداء

إلى روح أبي الذي علّمني أن العثرةَ طفره.

إلى روح أمّي التي غمرتني بدلالٍ لمْ يترُكْ لي بالمحبةِ حسره.

إلى روح أخي الكبير الذي فارقني على حينِ غرَّه.

إلى رفيقة دربي التي آزرتني في كلّ فكره.

إلى فِلذَاتِ الكبد الثلاث التي أكملت لي في الحياةِ أسره.

إلى كلْ من اكتسبَ من عاتياتِ الزمانِ عِبره.

Contents

ألمحتويات

Preface

My first poetic attempt was penned in the late fifties of the last century, during my final years in high school.

I set the pen aside when I entered medical school, but I did make some intermittent attempts on specific occasions and under the patronage of the church.

I picked up the pen again at the beginning of the second decade of the current century and continued to publish regularly on both alqosh.net and ankawa.com under the name "Sabah Kyya", along with modest contributions to literary festivals organized annually by The Chaldean Cultural Salon (Forum) in Windsor, Ontario and the solidarity ceremony arranged jointly by The Chaldean Voice Radio and Family Adoption Program in Detroit, Michigan.

I feel a special yearning to write poetic quartets. Perhaps, I was inspired when I started to knock on the door of poetry. I was introduced to the famous poetry quartets *Epic, Where Is My Right?* of the late Iraqi poet Mohammad Saleh Bahr Aluloom and other poetry quartets titled *Incantations* by the late Lebanese Immigrant poet Elia Abu Madi.

I preferred my book, which bears the name *Flashes of the Present Pain*, to be expressed in the motherland's language and the new homeland's language (North America). The poetry quartets are my nonliteral translation, while maintaining the meaning, drawn from the original Arabic text.

The Flashes include eight quartets, seven of which account, to some extent, for the pain suffered by the wounded motherland in general, and the ethnic minorities including Christians, Sabean Mandaeans and Yazidis in particular. These people have been marginalized and despised along with loss, despair, and deprivation of their rights, other than displacement, threat, intimidation and even death. The eighth quartet concludes the journey of the Flashes by recounting the suffering of my heart.

تمهيد

خط قلمي أولى محاولاتي الشعرية في نهاية خمسينات القرن الماضي خلال مرحلة دراستي الأعدادية.

أودعت القلم جانباً منذ دخولي كلية الطب إلا من بعض المحاولات المتقطعة بين فترات متباعدة في مناسبات محددة وبرعاية الكنيسة.

أمسكت القلم ثانية من غير ميعاد في بدء العقد الثاني من القرن الحالي لأنشر بانتظام بإسم « صباح قيّا» في موقعي ألقوش.نت وعنكاوة.كوم, مع مساهمات متواضعة في المهرجانات الأدبية الفنية التي ينظمها الصالون الثقافي الكلداني سنوياً في وندزر كندا, والحفل التضامني الذي أقامته إذاعة صوت الكلدان مع برنامج تبني عائلة في ديترويت أمريكا.

أشعر بميلٍ خاص لنظم الرباعيات الشعرية, ربما لتأثري عند طرقي باب الشعر بالرباعيات الشعرية الشهيرة ملحمة أين حقي للشاعر العراقي الراحل محمد صالح بحر العلوم, والرباعيات الشعرية الموسومة ألطلاسم للشاعر اللبناني المهجري الراحل إيليا أبو ماضي.

إرتأيت أن يتكلم نتاجي االذي يحمل إسم ومضات الألم الحاضر لغة الوطن الأم مع لغة الوطن الجديد (أمريكا الشمالية), والأخيرة هي ترجمتي غير الحرفية مع المحافظة على المعنى, والمستقاة من النص العربي للرباعيات.

تتضمن الومضات ثمان رباعيات تحكي في سبع منها جزءً يسيراً من الالم الذي لحق بالشعب الجريح عموماً وما جابهته ولا تزال الأقليات الإثنية من المسيحيين والصابئة المندائيين واليزيديين من تهميش واستصغار مقروناً بالضياع واليأس وسلب الحقوق عدا التشريد والتهديد والترويع وحتى زهق الأرواح وهتك الأعراض.
تختتم الرباعية الثامنة سفر الومضات بسرد ما أصاب قلبي من عذابات.

7

Acknowledgment

My thanks and appreciations go to my younger brother Tarik, who is a graduate of the Academy of Art, and to my youngest daughter Hiba, who is in her last year of high school, for their contribution with the illustrative sketches.

I would also thank my colleague Shatha Markus for reviewing the Arabic version of some of the poetry quartets.

Special thanks to Eva (The Fiverr Team, fiverr.com), who finalized the editing and grammar check of the English text.

شكر وتقدير

أتوجه بالشكر والامتنان إلى أخّي الأصغر طارق، وهو خريج أكاديمية الفنون الجميلة، وإلى ابنتي الصغرى هبة، التي هي في السنة الأخيرة من دراستها الثانوية، لمساهمتهما في الرسومات التوضيحية.

كما أشكر زميلتي شذى مرقوس لمراجعتها بعض الرباعيات الشعرية للجزء العربي من الكتاب.

شكر خاص للمحررة إيفا (من فريق فيفر عبر الإنترنيت) التي وضعت اللمسات الأخيرة لتنقيح النص الإنكليزي للكتاب من الناحية اللغوية والنحوية.

Monologue:
Where Are You?

مناجاة: أين أنتِ؟

Oh' Virgin Mary, the purest have come your way.
In your apparitions, you asked us to pray.
We will keep praying until we decay.
The echo of the rosary will waken those astray.

Mother, whatever I write is not new.
What has been said before proved to be true.
Your people are captives in the labyrinth of earth.
Oh' patron of creation, we ask you for a breath.
Where are you?

*****

We all walk to martyrdom for your sake.
Since carrying the crucifix banner, we wake.
The devil is blowing fire toward us.
The flame of evil is on the rise.
Where are you?

*****

Behold, the churches have been desolate.
The priests were terrified by the storm of hate.
The crosses were removed, and people left with injury.
The bells knocked in misery.
Where are you?

*****

أماهُ مهما كتبتُ لنْ آتيكِ بالجديدِ

فما قيلَ قبلَ اليوم لا يُجارى بالمزيدِ

شعبكِ في متاهاتِ الأرضِ يشقى كالعبيدِ

يا شفيعةَ الخَلْقِ أمَّ الوجودِ...أينِ أنتِ؟

*****

نحنُ مِنْ أجلكِ للشهادةِ جمعُنا يمضي

مذ حملنا رايةَ الصَلْبِ نشرناها بومْضِ

نفخَ الشيطانُ ناراً كيْ علينا هو يقضي

ولهيبُ الشرِّ يشتدُّ ويلْظي...أينَ أنتِ؟

*****

هَوَذا الكنائسُ صِرْحُها قد أمسى خرابا

أرعبوأ الكُهّان فيها وأذاقوهمْ عذابا

زِيلتْ الصلبانُ عنها أشبعوا الناسَ حِرابا

يقرعُ الناقوسُ في حزنٍ سرابا...أينَ أنتِ؟

*****

15

Panic is in every house or people are suffering from calamity.
A child screams for water, and the mother is in captivity.
The men of the suburbs are queued in agony each night.
The chains of humiliation cause the bleeding on sight.
Where are you?

*****

They entered the house of virgins and muddled its sanctuary.
Though they were minors, bedding them was compulsory.
What sort of religion sexes a carcass?
Oh' Mary,[1] how do we accept such trespass?
Where are you?

*****

What was erected for ages was ruined in minutes of abhorrence.
Who is going to believe the story of religion without evidence?
No buildings, no relics, not even codes.
They burned the symbols of the glorious words.
Where are you?

*****

هلعٌ في كلِّ دارٍ أو معاناةُ مصائبْ
طفلةٌ تصرخُ ماءً ونساءٌ لا تُجاوبْ
ورجالُ الحيِّ ليلاً في عذاباتٍ تناوبْ
وسياطُ الذلِّ تُدمي كلَّ جانبْ...أينَ أنتِ؟

*****

دخلوا دارَ العذارى واستباحوا حُرُماتهْ
قُصَّراً كُنَّ الصبايا تِلْكَ مِنْ صُلْبِ سِماتهْ
أيُّ دينٍ يختلي الجسمَ المُسَجَّى بِمماتهْ؟
كيفَ يا العذراءُ[1] نرضى بِزُناتهْ؟...أينَ أنتِ؟

*****

ما شادَ على الأرضِ سنيناً أفْنتْهُ دقائقْ
مَنْ سيحكي قصةَ الدينِ بتصويرِ الحقائقْ
لا بناءٌ لا رموزٌ لا ولا حتّى رقائقْ
أعدموا تاريخَ مجدٍ بحرائقْ...أينَ أنتِ؟

*****

17

We are not supposed to conquer invaders head by head.
We followed peaceful religion despite the waves of bloodshed.
How many martyrs embraced death by crucifixion?
The swords harvested priests and monks with no reaction.
Where are you?

*****

Never think the West will defend us or is positive.
The West does not support a religion without rewards.
His God is the dollar with an indifferent alternative.
Even Caesar[2] was not one of those kinds.
Where are you?

*****

We have no treasure but the glory of God.
We did not fight with a bullet or a sword.
How many innocent necks were chopped?
Bloody scenes were witnessed all over the world.
Where are you?

*****

نحنُ لا نقوى على قهرِ الغزاةِ بالمعاركْ
قد جَبَلْنا الدينَ سِلْماً رغمَ موجاتِ المهالكْ
كمْ شهيدٍ عانقَ الموتَ صليباً به ماسِكْ؟
وحصادُ السيفِ قسّيسٌ وناسِكْ...أينَ أنتِ؟

*****

لا نظُنُّ الغربَ عنّا في دِفاعٍ أو قتالِ
فَهْوَ لا يسْنُدُ ديناً لا يُجازيهِ بمالِ
دينُهُ الدولارُ حصراً ببديلٍ لا يبالي
لمْ يكُنْ قيصرُ[2] مِنْ هذي الخصالِ...أينَ أنتِ؟

*****

نحنُ لا نملُكُ غيرَ مجدِ الألهِ سلاحا
لمْ نُقاتِلْ برصاصٍ أو نبادلْهُمْ رماحا
كمْ رِقابٍ نُحِرَتْ جَهْراً فزادَتْها جراحا؟
دمُها السفيحُ يرويهِ سياحا...أينَ أنتِ؟

*****

19

Is it a sin if Christ, in our conscience, radiates?
Your Son won a cross; we are by His cross saved.
Our slapped left cheek calls the right for a similar hit.
In which religion does forgiveness fit?
Where are you?

*****

Two thousand years ago, we were baptized in Christ.
Thomas the apostle[3] came with the Gospel in his right hand.
With the bitter ages, the people scattered wide.
Who will heal the wounded motherland?[4]
Where are you?

*****

We have abandoned the precious country by force.
Some have achieved success, but more have faced loss.
The son distanced himself from his father to live as derelict.
The cruelty of living and the kindness are in conflict.
Where are you?

*****

ذنبُنا أنَّ المسيحَ في ثنايانا يَشِعُّ

إبنُكِ نالَ صليباً نحنُ للصلبان نَبْعُ

خدُّنا الأيمَنُ كالأيسرِ صَفْعاً لهُ يدعو

كمْ مِنَ الأديانِ للغفرانِ شَرْعُ؟...أينَ أنتِ؟

*****

قبلَ ألفيْنِ مِنَ اليوم تَعَمَّدْنا مسيحَ

جاءَنا توما الرسولُ³ دَلَّنا الدربَ الصحيحَ

ومعَ بغيِ الزمانِ أصبحَ الشعبُ شحيحَ

منْ يُداوي الوطنَ الأمَّ الجريحَ؟...أينَ أنتِ؟

*****

قد هجرنا البلدَ الغالي⁴ بأسمالِ المتاعِ

بعضُنا لاقى نجاحاً والكثيرُ في ضَياعِ

تركَ الأبنُ أباهُ وتوارى في البقاعِ

قسوةُ العيْشِ وقلبٌ في صراعِ...أينَ أنتِ؟

*****

21

Do we leave the faith or stay firm on it?
Who else confronted the lion with a fist?
Despite the hatred yelling for more shed,
The faithful glorified their dreadful end.
Where are you?

*****

Oh' Virgin Mary, the purest have come your way.
In your apparitions, you asked us to pray.
We will keep praying until we decay.
The echo of the rosary will waken those astray.
Where are you?

*****

It does not matter if we miss your elegant stature.
Loving the Virgin is part of our nature.
All that we call on is mercy to the lost.
The injustice of today is torturing most.
Where are you?

*****

يا تُرى هل نترُكُ الأيمانَ أمْ نبقى عليْه؟
مَنْ سِوانا جابَهَ الليْثَ براحاتِ يديْهِ؟
وعويلُ الحقدِ للأجسادِ أنْ تُرمى إليْهِ
مَجَّدَتْ والطُعْمُ يُلهي ساعِدَيْهِ...أينَ أنتِ؟

*****

مريمُ العذراءُ يا أسمى النساءِ الطاهراتِ
قد ظهرتِ في زمانٍ ودعوتِ للصلاةِ
سيُصَلّي اليومَ حيٌّ أمْ مُساقٌ للمماتِ
وصدى التسبيحِ يدوي للخطاةِ...أينَ انتِ؟

*****

نحنُ لا ننشُدُ أنْ نبصُرَ قواماً بَهيّا
صورةُ العذراءِ بالقلبِ وبالأفكارِ تحيا
كلُّ ما ندعوهُ رحماكِ لمَنْ صارَ شقيّا
وغدى الجورُ على الدهرِ عتيّا...أينَ أنتِ؟

*****

23

Suffering,
To Whom Do I Complain?

معاناة: لمن أشتكي؟

I am in the cradle of civilization. Babylon is my land.

Mosul's[5] cross is bleeding. To whom do I complain?
The churches of Christ are destroyed with bombs.
Our people are homeless with no water to drain,
Exclaiming, "Allah Akbar!" for slaughtering the souls.
To whom do I complain?

*****

What kind of god opens a brothel and calls it heaven?
Earning the entering price through extermination.
The suicidal will enjoy great sex once getting in.
He does not care if the victim is a boy or maiden.
To whom do I complain?

*****

The sword is hanging on the neck. To whom do I complain?
Either to be Muslim or pay tribute from your earnings.
Or leaving your land, never thinking of returning.
Those who disobey will be slain.
To whom do I complain?

*****

لمن أشتكي والموصلُ⁵ صليبُها ينزفُ؟
وكنائسُ المسيح بقنابلٍ تُقذفُ
وشعبنا بلا مأوىً ولا ماءٍ يرتشفُ
والله أكبرُ في ذبحه يغلو ويسرفُ
لمن أشتكي؟

*****

أيُّ ربٍ يفتحُ مبغىً ويدعوه بجنّه؟
يجني أثمانَ الدخولِ من إباداتٍ ومحنه
يحلمُ المؤمنُ فيها وطءَ أجسادٍ مِجنّه
لا يبالي من يضاجعْ حسنٌ كان أم فِتنه
لمن أشتكي؟

*****

لمن أشتكي والسيفُ بالأعناقِ معلّقٌ؟
تدخلُ الإسلامَ أم جزيةً مما تُسترزقُ
أو الرحيلَ عدا ما الجبينُ له يعرقُ
والموتُ لمن يعصي الشروطَ حتماً محققٌ
لمن أشتكي؟

*****

29

The mother does not breastfeed.
They stole her baby, and its wailing does not vanish.
With a wound, the father is grieved.
A stranger in the nearby suburb enjoys their anguish.
To whom do I complain?

*****

Tel Kaif[6] is irrigated with the inhabitant's' tears.
Baghdeda[7] is remembering Tikrit's[8] invasions with fear.
Telleskuf[9] witnessed death in the enclosures.
Bakufa[10] is narrating the beating of her armless defenders.
To whom do I complain?

*****

The spring of faith was almost broken.
God saved Alqosh[11] from the slayer folk.
Some groups reacted like a firm lock.
Others were entrenched with the people of Dohuk.[12]
To whom do I complain?

*****

لمن أشتكي والأُمُّ من ثديها لا تُرضعُ؟
سرقوا الطفولةِ وعويلُها لا ينفعُ
وعلى الثرى أبٌ من جرحهِ يتوجّعُ
وفي الحيّ غريبٌ بعذابهم يستمتعُ
لمن أشتكي؟

*****

لمن أشتكي وتلكيفُ[6] تُسقى دمعَ أهليها؟
وبغديدا[7] تبصرُ غزواتِ تكريت[8] ماضيها
وتلّسقفْ[9] شهدتْ أقفاصاً مات من فيها
وباقوفة[10] تحكي ضربَ من صدَّ دينَ غازيها
لمن أشتكي؟

*****

لمن أشتكي ونبعُ الإيمانِ كاد أن يُخرقْ؟
تلك ألقوشُ[11] نجاها اللهُ غزوةَ الفُسّقْ
أبى من أبنائها إلا أن يحرس كالبيدقْ
وجموعُها الأخرى بأهلِ دهوك[12] تتخندقْ
لمن أشتكي؟

*****

31

The agony is wandering around in the villages:
No buildings, no houses, no smiling visages.
The wound in everyone is still fresh red.
Is there a solution nearby for the bloodshed?
To whom do I complain?

*****

The game is wrapped with mystery and secrets.
How do a few thousand outsiders conquer a trained military force?
The army did not fight a battle, betraying the covenant.
He fled like a mouse hiding in corners and holes
To whom do I complain?

*****

How often do I complain? No one will pay attention.
It is an age of self-interest; people have no respect.
The decision-makers will reject differing comments.
Though turning the white into black, they throw accusations.
To whom do I complain?

*****

لمن أشتكي وفي قرانا يسرحُ الألمُ؟
لا بناءٌ لا ديارٌ لا وجوه تبتسمُ
كلُّ من تلقاه جراحُهُ ليس تلتئمُ
متى الحلولُ والأشهرُ تمضي تتقدمُ
لمن أشتكي؟

*****

لمن أشتكي واللعبةُ أسرارٌ وخفايا؟
بضعَّ آلافٍ دخيلٍ يغنمُ كلَّ السرايا
لم يخضْ جيشٌ قتالاً نكثَ عهدَ الوصايا
فرَّ مذعوراً كفأرٍ يحتمي جحرَ الزوايا
لمن أشتكي؟

*****

لمن أشتكي وشكوايَ لن تلقَ اهتماما؟
هو عصرُ المصالح ليس للمرء احتراما
عند صنّاع القرارِ يفقدُ الرأيُ التزاما
يقلبُ الأبيضَ أسودْ ثمَّ يرمينا اتهاما
لمن أشتكي؟

*****

Behold, the world is exhausted by various hoaxes.
Some countries enjoy prosperity, while others suffer losses.
The politician's' game is sinning expressed in an angel's character,
Claiming the truth openly, but deeply it's slander.
To whom do I complain?

*****

Who is the one who draws the way for nature?
Every foot in the East is burned by torture.
Justice is sunk into the depths of seawater.
The breath is muffled by despair, for air is eager.
To whom do I complain?

*****

Oh' West, why do you favor who pays more?
You even support a hypocrite; his pockets, you adore.
Do you think the rule is monopoly, forgetting the days of lashing out?
Whoever lives on the earth will one day turn into ash.
To whom do I complain?

*****

هوذا العالمُ منهوكٌ بأنواع المهازلْ
دولٌ تنعمُ جاهاً ودويلاتٌ تقاتلْ
لعبةُ الساسة آثامٌ بأقوال فضائلْ
تدّعي الحقَّ جهاراً ثمَّ تنحرهُ بباطلْ
لمن أشتكي؟

*****

يا تُرى من ذا الذي يرسمُ للكون طريقا؟
كلُّ شبرٍ في ربوع الشرق يلتظُّ حريقا
غرق العدلُ وغاص في المحيطات عميقا
كتم الأنفاسَ باليأس زفيراً وشهيقا
لمن أشتكي؟

*****

أيها الغربُ لماذا في الموازين تحابي؟
تنصرُ من ترتأيه حتى لو كان مرابي
هل تظن الحكمَ حكراً نتسى أيام الحسابِ؟
كلُّ من بالأرض حيٌّ سوف يمضي للترابِ
لمن أشتكي؟

*****

35

I do not deny living in a country of equality.
All the people are the same whatever their ethnicity.
The power of law is applicable despite their diversity.
Anyone with wrongdoings deserves a penalty.
To whom do I complain?

*****

I am worried about an action based on the pillars of civilization
That opens the doors to sectors infested with treachery,
Spreads sedition openly, hates even masonry.
Beware the newcomers transmitting the contamination.
To whom do I complain?

*****

Oh' West, when are you going to wake up from sleep?
The cells of hatred in the mosques are digging deep.
Today, they are in a dormant role implanting bloody seeds.
By that time, there's no benefit of remorse for ignoring the heeds.
To whom do I complain?

*****

أنا لا أنكرُ عيشي في ثناياك كريما
لا تفرّقْ بين شكاكٍ بربٍ أو قويما
سلطةُ القانونِ تقتصُ سفيهاً أو حكيما
كلَّ من خالف في فعله عرفاً مستقيما
لمن أشتكي؟

*****

جلُّ خوفي من صنيعٍ باسم أركان الحضاره
يفتح الباب لقومٍ جبُلَ الغدرَ خياره
ينشرُ الفتنةَ جهراً يكره حتى الحجاره
إحذروا القادمَ كالنعجة من تلك القذاره
لمن أشتكي؟

*****

أيها الغربُ متى عن غيّك تصحو وتفيقْ؟
وخلايا الحقد في المساجدِ تختطُّ الطريقْ
يومها في دورِ سباتٍ لغدٍ دامٍ محيقْ
عندها لن يجدِ نفعاً ندمٌ أو لوم صديقْ
لمن أشتكي؟

*****

Oh' West, do you know that is a religion of betrayal?
Hundreds of its verses call for killing non-Muslims.
Every caliph was assassinated by pushy disloyal.
The stab of the dagger was the prayer's custom.
To whom do I complain?

*****

How often I wished to go back to my mother country.
It is like a fragrant rose despite the thorns of a prairie.
Though its sweet tastes bitter, no other place is my flavor.
The thrill of a lover is when the heart heats like cinder.
To whom do I complain?

*****

In the diaspora, I lost the keys of boasting.
I became a loser in a world of gambling, though not gaming.
The pressure of life is so hard. How long do I try?
Wishing myself to be a bird, free to fly.
To whom do I complain?

*****

أيها الغربُ أتعلمْ إنه دينُ الخيانه؟
تدعو آياتُهُ قتلاً مائةٌ غير الإهانه
كلُّ من صار خليفه زال بالغدر كيانه
طعنةُ الخنجرِ تُدمي بعد إعلان الأذانه
لمن أشتكي؟

*****

كم تمنيتُ زماناً أن اعود لدياري
فهيَ كالوردة عبقٌ رغم أشواك البراري
مرُّها حلوُ المذاقِ وسواها لا أجاري
متعةُ العاشقِ أن يُكوى بجمرٍ أو بنارِ
لمن أشتكي؟

*****

أنا في المهجرِ ضيعتُ مفاتيح المفاخرْ
صرت كالمهزوم في دنيا القمارِ لا يقامرْ
أرنو على بلدٍ ضاق بي كي منه أهاجرْ
أرمق في العلياءِ بشوقٍ جنحَ كلَّ طائرْ
لمن أشتكي؟

*****

39

How can I forget my love? To whom do I owe my loyalty?
The Iraqi roots are soaked with water of originality.
I'm very nostalgic, no matter how long the dispersion.
They are the genes inherited by offspring in succession.
To whom do I complain?

*****

I am the son of two rivers: Tigris and Euphrates.[13]
I ran away from those who were reluctant to provide food.
No safety, no harmony, and they ruined the brotherhood.
They favor the ignorant, but ignore the intelligent.
To whom do I complain?

*****

Oh' my heart, why you are yearning for torture?
Stop beating for what was yesterday a savior.
It is in labor today, giving birth to a scrounger.
And its tears stinging the cheeks with tinder.
To whom do I complain?

*****

كيف تنسوني حبيباً أعشقُ حتى الثماله؟
فالعراقيُ جذورٌ يرتوي ماءَ الأصاله
نفسي تشتدُّ حنيناً في الشتاتِ مهما طاله
هيَ جيناتٌ ورثناها تباعاً من سلاله
لمن أشتكي؟

*****

أنا إبنُ الرافدينْ دجلةُ والفراتُ[13] مائي
هربت بالأمسِ ممن يحجمُ اليومَ إيوائي
لا أمانٌ لا وئامٌ مسخَ معنى الإخاءِ
يشتري الجاهلَ كي يقصي أصحابَ الذكاءِ
لمن أشتكي؟

*****

أتظلُّ يا فؤادي للعذاباتِ مشتاقا؟
كفاك خفقاً على من كان بالأمسِ عراقا
وهو اليومُ مخاضٌ لغدٍ يولدُ عاقا
ودموعٌ تلسعُ الخدَّ لهيباً واحتراقا
لمن أشتكي؟

*****

I am in the cradle of civilizations.[14] Babylon[15] is my land.
The treachery of the Persians[16] blended the blood with mud.
A cross appeared on the horizon and all gathered to pray.
They preached peace on earth, enlightened the salvation way.
To whom do I complain?

*****

I belong to Jesus. This is my pride and honor.
Which religion is asking forgiveness for sadistic invaders?
It is the one that evangelizes loving your opponent.
And when someone slaps your right cheek, present the left.
To whom do I complain?

*****

To whom do I complain when no one answers my yell?
Is it a sin to follow a religion that calls for the love of an antagonist?
I will become a martyr on the earth, not entering hell.
How often do we continue to pay the price of faith without limit?
To whom do I complain?

*****

أنا مهدُ الحضاراتِ[14] بابلُ[15] أصلي وفصلي
غدرَ الفرسُ[16] بها مزجوا الدماءَ بوحلِ
لاح في الأفقِ صليبٌ هرع الجمعُ يصلّي
بشّرَ الناسَ على الأرضِ سلاماً لا بقتلِ
لمن أشتكي؟

*****

أنا أتباعُ المسيح هذا فخري واعتزازي
أيُّ دينٍ يطلبُ العفوَ لبطّاشٍ وغازي؟
غير من قال بحقٍ لغريمٍ لا تجازي
خدك الأيمنُ بالصفعِ لثانيه موازي
لمن أشتكي؟

*****

لمن أشتكي وصراخي صدىً لن يلقى مجيبْ؟
ذنبي من دينٍ ينادي حبَّ عدوٍ كالقريبْ
أغدو شهيداً بأرضٍ كي في السماءِ لي نصيبْ
كم نظلُّ ندفع الأثمانَ طوعاً دون حسيبْ؟
لمن أشتكي؟

*****

43

I leave the matter to the Lord, with my concern.
It is not the first time we have been threatened to wane.
The Almighty will release our shackles and show us the way.
From him we seek salvation. To him I scream with pain.
To whom do I complain?

*****

أتركُ الأمرَ لربٍ إنه مجدُ الأعالي

ليست المرةُ الأولى أن نهددْ بالزوالِ

هو من يفرجُ ضيقاً يقلبُ حالاً بحالٍ

منه نرتجي خلاصاً لهُ أبغي بسؤالي

لمن أشتكي؟

*****

A cross appeared on the horizon and all gathered to pray.

Calling:
Whom Do I Call?

مُناداة: مَنْ أنادي؟

Tarik Mikhael
2019

In Sumer, we invented the writing.
A new invasion prevailed called ISIS.
Young girls followed them from Marrakesh to Damascus.
Seeking paradise from the act of trespasses.

My tears are for people from my wounded homeland
Whose elite fled and the wound's depth rose.
Indifferent of being lonely and showing no remorse.
Though facing hardship and deeply feeling sad.
Whom do I call?

*****

Since we betrayed the king, we are rivals to each other.
We praised all the rulers, then we stripped them up forever.
How often did we drag out the innocent but applaud the sinner?
We did not distinguish between tyrant and forgiver.
Whom do I call?

*****

Those manners are strange to our inherited customs.
We as a nation used to live as loving blossoms.
All the sectors were flooded with sweetness.
Why are they now doubting and suspicious?
Whom do I call?

*****

دمعي على وطني الجريح بأهله يشقى
صفْوُهُ فرَّ طريداً زادَ مِنْ جُرحِهِ عُمقا
هامَ في سوحِ الضياعِ لا يبالي ما سيلقى
مِنْ صِعابٍ تجعلُ الإنسانَ رِقًّا...مَنْ أنادي؟

*****

نحنُ مُذْ غدرنا الملكَ المُفَدَّى في تناحرْ
نصطفي منْ يعتلينا ثمَّ نُلقيهِ خسائرْ
كمْ سحلنا كمْ قتلنا كمْ هتفنا لِمُكابِرْ
لمْ نُمَيّزْ بينَ بطاشٍ وغافِرْ...منْ أنادي؟

*****

تلكُمُ الأخلاقُ عنْ أعرافِ ماضينا غريبه
نحنُ شعبٌ ألفَ العيشَ حبيباً وحبيبه
غمرتْ أطيافُهُ الأمسَ موداتٍ وطيبه
ما دهاها اليوم في شكٍ وريبه؟...منْ أنادي؟

*****

Since the birth of civilization on the land of beauty.
The crown was given to those with integrity.
The throne was ousted by six waves of atrocity.
The people resisted those who were against their entity.
Whom do I call?

*****

In Sumer,[17] we invented the writing.
In Babylon,[18] we constructed what nature is lacking.
To Assyria,[19] all the kingdoms bowed their heads.
How do we accept those relics to be shreds?
Whom do I call?

*****

It is not a shame to restore the glory of our ancient past.
From past lessons, the new era glitters bright.
The days of evil will not return.
By tomorrow, the happiness will shine again.
Whom do I call?

*****

منذُ ميلادِ الحضاراتِ على أرضي الجميله
ألْقتْ ريادةُ العرشِ بأقوامٍ أصيله
غدرتها ستُّ موجاتٍ أرادتها ذليله
قاومَ الأصلُ مفاهيماً بديله...منْ أنادي؟

*****

نحنُ في سومرَ[17] كتبناها حروفاً بديعه
وفي بابلَ[18] شيّدنا ما تضاهيه الطبيعه
ومنْ آشورَ[19] أجبرنا المَمالكَ أنْ تطيعَ
كيفَ للآثارِ تلكَ أنْ تضيعَ؟...منْ أنادي؟

*****

ليسَ عيبٌ أنْ نعيدَ مجدَ ماضينا التليدَ
فمنَ الماضي دروسٌ ترفدُ العصرَ الجديدَ
خيرةُ الأقوامِ يوماً لشرورٍ لنْ تعيدَ
تتبنى للغدِ شعباً سعيدَ...منْ أنادي؟

*****

55

We, in history, do not forget the Mongol's'[20] genocide.
They shut up a million souls; more went into hiding.
The water blended with blood, and the massacre got worse.
With the sunrise, the people returned to rejoice.
Whom do I call?

*****

Throughout the ages, we suffered from neighbors and strangers.
Friends in the harvest, in their depth, competitors.
They emptied out all the treasures.
A curse came upon those robbers.
Whom do I call?

*****

A new invasion prevailed called ISIS.[21]
They justified the killing according to the verses.
Young girls followed them from Marrakesh[22] to Damascus.[23]
Seeking paradise from the act of trespasses.
Whom do I call?

*****

نحنُ في التاريخِ لا ننسى إباداتِ المغولِ[20]
أسكتوا مليونَ نفسٍ أحرقوا ذُخْرَ العقولِ
مزجوا الماءَ دماءً بصراخٍ وعويلِ
بزغَ الفجرُ فعدنا للأصولِ...منْ أنادي؟

*****

سطوةُ الدهرِ علينا من غريبٍ وقريبٍ
أصدقاءٌ في الحصادِ غرماءٌ في القلوبِ
أفرغوا ما في الكنوزِ ملؤوا كلَّ الجيوبِ
نقمةٌ حلَّتْ على هذي الشعوبِ...منْ أنادي؟

*****

جاءنا غزوٌ جديدٌ أطلقوا إسمَهُ داعشْ[21]
أعلنَ القتلَ حلالاً وهْوَ عنْ دينِه طائشْ
لحقَتْهُ فتياتٌ لدمشقَ[22] منْ مراكشْ[23]
تبتغي الجنةَ مِنْ فعلِ الفواحِشْ...مَنْ أنادي؟

*****

57

They launched genocide under Caliphate rule.
Killing in the name of God which showed Almighty as a myth.
If the Lord's religion is really cruel,
Atheism will be preached all over the earth.
Whom do I call?

*****

What kind of religion considers slaughtering a message of God?
What pious people claims cutting the neck is an order from the Lord?
What kind of heaven opens its doors for perverts,
Eagerly looking for sex with young boys and mermaids?
Whom do I call?

*****

Baghdad[24] has witnessed invasion after invasion;
Each time it withstood the cruelty of oppression.
Even though Hulagu[25] authorized one of the worst carnages,
The conditions later returned to a normal range.
Whom do I call?

*****

شنّوا الإبادةَ جمعاً باسم أحكامِ الخلافه
ألصقوا باللهِ فكراً يُظهرُ الربَ خُرافه
لو إلهٌ يبعثُ الدينَ آياتٍ سَيّافه
نُبشّرُ الكفرَ في كلِّ مسافه...مَنْ أنادي؟

*****

أيُّ دينٍ يحسبُ النحرَ مِنَ الله رساله؟
أيُّ نفسٍ تقطعُ الرأسَ وتدعوهُ عداله؟
أيُّ خُلْدٍ يفتحُ البابَ لأرذالٍ حُثاله؟
تشتهي الغلمانَ والحورَ وصالَ...مَنْ انادي؟

*****

شهدتْ بغدادُ[24] منذُ البدءِ غزواتٍ عديده
لمْ تكُنْ وقتاً كهذي قسوةُ البطشِ شديده
حتّى هولاكو[25] أباحَ فترةً غيرِ مديده
عادتْ الأحوالُ آمالاً رشيده...مَنْ انادي؟

*****

What has been said two thousand years ago has been proven true today:
The inhabitants were forcibly evicted and went astray.
Their only guilt is carrying the cross and glorifying the Lord.
Oh' God, how long it takes to depose the rule of a sword?
Whom do I call?

*****

What had been recently observed is not our manners.
My country had been infested by waves of intruders.
No insider recognized the Mongol or the Jihadi.[26]
Woe to the falsity of the nicknamed al-Baghdadi.[27]
Whom do I call?

*****

How long does the wound remains untreated?
If it stays long, it will lead us toward annihilation.
The burden of diseases arrives when left without medication.
The stopping of bleeding is constantly needed.
Whom do I call?

*****

ما قيلَ منذُ ألفينِ قد غدى اليومَ حقيقه
طردوا السكانَ قَسْراً سرقوا حتى الوثيقه
ذنبُهُمْ حملُ صليب مجدُهُ ربُّ الخليقه
كمْ يدومُ جرمٌ شُذّاذٌ صفيقه؟...مَنْ أنادي؟

*****

ما عهدناهُ حديثاً لم يكُنْ صُنْعَ بلادي
فبلادي وطأتها غربةٌ بسم الجهادِ²⁶
لمْ تبايعها القفارُ لا ولا حتى البوادي
تبّاً منْ زيّفَ كُنْيَةَ البغدادي²⁷...مَنْ أنادي؟

*****

كمْ يظلُّ الجرحُ من دون علاجٍ وشفاءٍ؟
فهْوَ لو باتَ طويلاً قادنا نحو الفناءِ
وطأةُ الأمراضِ أنْ تُترَكَ من غيرِ دواءِ
جُرحنا نزفُهُ فاقَ كلَّ داءٍ...مَنْ انادي؟

*****

61

Where is conscience? Is the world really comatose?
Or is it secretly dancing, getting friendly with the perpetrators?
How does an army fail to repel a few thousand invaders?
Leaving the land without showing remorse.
Whom do I call?

*****

Invasion, invasion, invasion, and invasion!
Burning, destruction, killing, and ablation.
Pleasing the invaders before facing death.
The generations never abandoned the earth.
Whom do I call?

*****

The illusion-filled minds thought invasion was intelligence.
With the rising of the sun, God revealed their ignorance.
How can they conquer the seven billions of the world?
The awakening of the universe will rid such mold.
Whom do I call?

*****

أين الضميرُ هلِ العالمُ حقاً في سباتِ؟
أم لها يرقصُ سراً وهْوَ خِلٌّ للجناةِ؟
لمْ يطقْ جيشٌ يديه صدَّ آلافِ الغزاةِ
ترَك الأرضَ وغابَ في الفلاةِ...مَنْ أنادي؟

*****

غزَواتٌ غزَواتٌ غزَواتٌ غزَواتٌ
ثمَّ حرقٍ ودمار وبالناسِ نكاياتْ
تُطربُ الغازيَ حيناً بعداً يطويها المماتُ
تُروى للأجيالِ عنها حكاياتٌ...مَنْ أنادي؟

*****

ملأَ الوهمُ عقولاً ظنّت الغزوَ ذكاءَ
ومع صبحٍ منيرٍ يكشفُ اللهُ الغباءَ
كيف تقوى أن تكيدَ سبعَ مليارٍ عداءَ؟
سيفيقُ الكونُ يرميها هباءَ...مَنْ أنادي؟

*****

63

The wave of today's hatred muddles the world.
Ask history about the genocides of the past;
Previous calamities proved worse than the last.
All who draw the sword will die by the sword.[28]
Whom do I call?

*****

What we see today is a dream or the beginning of Rupture.
Revelation of John[29] refers to Babylon as the start.
It will be divided into three. This is the symbolic account.
A King will bring the peace, ending human torture.
Whom do I call?

*****

موجةُ الحقدِ أتتنا بالغدِ حتماً سترحَلْ

إسألوا التاريخَ عنها يعلمُ ما قد سيحصَلْ

نكَباتٌ سابقاتٌ لم تكنْ من هذي أفضلْ

كلُّ منْ جاءَ بسيفٍ بهِ يُقتَلْ[28]...مَنْ أنادي؟

*****

ما نراهُ اليومَ حلماً أمْ علاماتِ النهايه

رؤيا يوحنا[29] تشيرُ بابلَ هي البدايه

تقسمُ إلى ثلاثٍ إنها رمزُ الحكايه

ومليكٌ يحملُ السلمَ برايه...مَنْ أنادي؟

*****

Questionings:
Who Is To Blame?

تساؤلات: مَنْ يُلاما؟

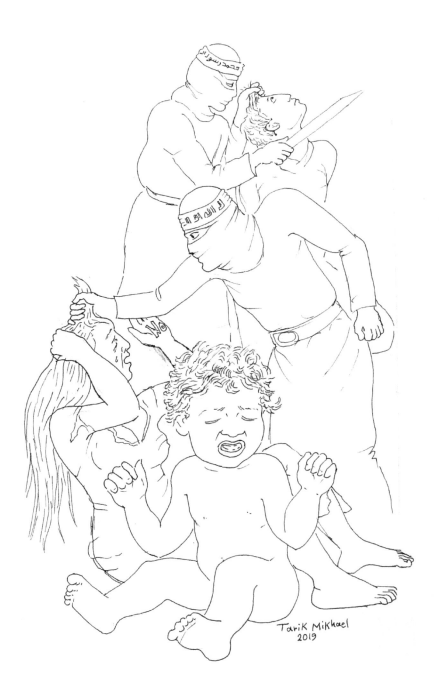

Slaughter, rape, and others are motionless.
A child screams and everyone around him is earless.
A mother is enslaved in the embrace of lust.
A father defies conversion despite the cut.

Is any one awake in Iraq or is everyone snoring?
The morning sun looks like a black mist.
Is the country lost or have the people forgotten their stint?
All the positions are filled by whoever is sinning.
Who is to blame?

*****

The country is split between rivalry sectors:
The Sunni[30] is not satisfied by who is in power.
The Shiite[31] does not believe that he is the ruler.
We are between those farces like caricatures.
Who is to blame?

*****

Slaughter, rape, and others are motionless.
A child screams and everyone around him is earless.
A mother is enslaved in the embrace of lust.
A father defies conversion despite the cut.
Who is to blame?

*****

هل في العراق صاحٍ أم الكلُّ نُوَّمُ؟
شمس الصباح كأنها غيمٌ أعتمُ
وطنٌ ضاع أم شعبٌ نسى ما يلزمُ؟
في كلِّ المناصبِ سارقٌ أو آثمُ
من يُلاما؟

*****

بلدٌ من التناحرِ يتشرذمُ
سنيٌّ[30] لا يرضى من به يتحكمُ
وشيعيٌّ[31] لم يصدق أنه الحَكَمُ
ونحن بين هذي المهازلِ نُثرَمُ
من يُلاما؟

*****

ذبحٌ واغتصابٌ وجمعٌ يتألمُ
طفلٌ برغمِ الصراخِ مَنْ حَوله أَصَمُ
أمٌ بأحضانِ الشهوةِ تُقتسمُ
وأبٌ حتى بالسيفِ لا يتأسلمُ
من يُلاما؟

*****

71

Why is the fire blazing in the ancestors' land?
Why is the cup of bitterness and poison at hand?
Why is the nation's cemetery destroyed with hooves?
Why are the rights of people buried in the grooves?
Who is to blame?

*****

I wish somebody could inspire in my wounded homeland.
When can I see our men willing to work side by side?
I wish there was a party that could unite the whole nation.
I wish there was a national banner in progression.
Who is to blame?

*****

During which era do we cry and pay condolence?
In every age, we have consolation and solace.
Forgetting the sadness of yesterday, and looking for the joy of today,
Proved that the present is like the past: dark clay.
Who is to blame?

*****

لِمَ النيرانُ في أرضِ الجدودِ تُضرمُ؟
وكأسُ المرارةِ يُحتسى والعلقمُ؟
وقبورُ قومي بالحوافرِ تُهدمُ؟
وحقوقُ شعبي بالمزابلِ تُردمُ؟
من يُلاما؟

*****

لو كان في وطني الجريحِ مَنْ يُلهمُ
ورجالُ عنهم أعمالٌ تتكلمُ
وأحزابٌ تجمعُ الشعبَ له تخدمُ
ورايةٌ بين الصفوفِ تتقدمُ
من يُلاما؟

*****

عنْ أيِّ عصرٍ نبكي نترحمٌ؟
في كل عصرٍ لنا عزاءٌ ومأتمُ
نطويَ الأمسَ عسى اليومُ نتنعمُ
فإذا الحاضرُ كالماضي ليلٌ أظلمُ
من يُلاما؟

73

Oh' World, you do not see! It's as if you are a dummy.
Despite all the victims, you are standing as an effigy.
Where is the conscience of the committed West?
Have we been together as a Christian sect?
Who is to blame?

*****

My homeland, I know more than what the others over there know.
Whoever has left that path is surely in the safest row.
Why stay and have your rocks be soaked with blood?
How many martyrs are entombed in the ground?
Who is to blame?

*****

My homeland, they call me Dhimmi[32] and so does my family.
Threatening with the sword is their homily.
The source of legislation is a clergy with turbans.
All the articles of the constitution are based on the Quran.[33]
Who is to blame?

*****

عالَمٌ لنْ تبصرَ كأنك دممُ
تلك الضحايا وأنت واقفٌ صنمُ
أين الضميرُ أيها الغربُ الملتزمُ؟
ونحنُ معاً بالمسيحية نِعَمُ
من يُلاما ؟

*****

بلادي أنا ممن هنالكَ أعلمُ
منْ غادرَ قبلاً دربُهُ حتماً أسلمُ
لِمَ البقاءُ والصخرُ فيكِ مُدممُ؟
كمْ شهيدٍ بعد شهيدٍ أمساً أعدمُ؟
من يُلاما ؟

*****

بلادي أنا ذميٌّ[32] وأهلي ذِممٌ
ما دام التسبيحُ بالنحْرِ هو العَلَمُ
ومصدرُ التشريعِ سيدٌ مُعممُ
ومنَ القرآنِ[33] نقرأُ نتعلمُ
من يُلاما ؟

*****

75

My homeland, you will flourish with secularism.
Justice will shadow every human organism.
No one religion is superior to another religion,
And the doctrines will have no division.
Who is to blame?

*****

My homeland, you are in my dream.
For you, I suffer and scream.
You are inspiring me to fame.
My tears are hot as a flame.
Who is to blame?

*****

بلادي بالعلمانيةِ تحيا تدُمُ
هيَ العدالةُ بِظلّها ننتظمُ
لا دينٌ يعلو على دينٍ ويختصمُ
ولا المذاهبُ ببعضها تَحتدمُ
من يُلاما ؟

*****

بلادي مِنَ العُشقِ أذوبُ وأحلمُ
هيَ في فؤادي حبيسةٌ تلتحمُ
هيَ في عقلي مُلهِمةٌ تتعظمُ
وأنا المهاجرُ بدمعي أستَحِمُ
من يُلاما ؟

*****

77

My Beloved Homeland

وطني الحبيب

80

My homeland, do not blame the one who intends to travel,
Nor who pulled the backpack to settle.
The freedom of human is an indispensible target;
It can not be bought or sold in the market.

You who lies in my captive heart.
You who coheres in my instinct.
Darkness looms from broken light,
As if the light is afraid to glint.

*****

A tongue inundated me with false promises.
My heart, from the flow of sadness, burst into pieces.
My eyes flooded the river with tears.
My entrails melted the rocks with sears.

*****

My beloved, who betrayed the covenant and landed?
Am I, from the ecstasy of migration, muddled?
I thought living in diaspora is pleasure,
And the mirage of the desert is water.

*****

My homeland, do not blame the one who intends to travel,
Nor who pulled the backpack to settle.
The freedom of human is an indispensible target;
It can not be bought or sold in the market.

*****

أيّها الراقدُ في قلبي الأسيرْ
أيّها السارحُ في عقلي الهجيرْ
ظلامٌ يلوحُ عنْ ضوءٍ كسيرْ
كأنَّ الضياءَ تخشى أنْ تُنيرْ

*****

لسانُ سقاني وعداً وغدرْ
فؤادي من زَحْمةِ الحزنِ انفجرْ
عينايَ من دمعِها فاضَ النهرْ
أحشائي من جمْرِها ذاب الصخرْ

*****

حبيبي مَنْ خانَ العهدَ فهجرْ؟
أم أنا مِن نشوةِ الهجرِ سكرْ؟
ظننتُ العيشَ في المهجرِ دُرَرْ
وخلتُ سراب الصحراءِ مطرْ

*****

وطني لا تلُمْ من ينوي السفرْ
منْ شدَّ الرحالَ أيضاً واستقرْ
حريّةُ الإنسانِ أسمى وطَرْ
لا تباعُ أو تُشْترى بِمَهَرْ

*****

83

In the diaspora you taste the sweetness of expression,
You denounce blasphemy or criticize religion.
The President is questioned ahead of the Minister,
The law is for the justice pillar.

*****

In the diaspora, you are free to choose.
It is sold from the meat even gammon,
And poured in the cup all sorts of alcoholic drink.
No prohibition or Islamic canon.

*****

My homeland, in the name of liberation, you are lost.
On the foreign tanks cohorts were brought.
Half of them thieves, the other hired pals.
They own everything apart from morals.

*****

My homeland, you have been sold by semi-humans.
Your charisma sunk into the depths of the sea.
Is there hope for Iraq to be?
Simulating the beauty of moon and sun.

*****

في المهجرِ يُذاقُ طعمُ التعبيرْ
يُنقدُ الدينُ أو يُشجَبُ التكفيرْ
يُساءلُ الرئيسُ قبلَ الوزير
ما دامَ القانونُ للعدلِ ظهيرْ

*****

في المهجرِ حريّةُ التخييرْ
يباعُ منَ اللحمِ حتى الخنزيرْ
تُصبُّ في الكأسِ أنواعُ الخميرْ
لا حرامٌ ولا في الشرعِ تجبيرْ

*****

وطني أضاعتك باسم التحرير
شلّةٌ على الدبابةِ تسيرْ
نصفها سارقٌ والآخرْ أجيرْ
مَلَكَتْ كلَّ شيءٍ إلّا الضميرْ

*****

وطني باعتكَ أشباهُ البشرْ
ورسمُكَ غاصَ في عمقِ البحرْ
فهلْ للعراقِ من بعدٍ صوَرْ؟
يحاكي سحرُها الشمسَ والقمرْ

*****

My homeland, I love you to the utmost.
I adorned you with a silky necklace.
I forgot the impact of a bitter life sort.
I keep seeing you as a charming princess.

*****

My homeland, you are my honor.
You stay in my sentiment forever.
I will ask God to enlighten your misery state,
And to return you back as you were: great.

*****

وطني أحببتك حبَّ القديرْ
وسمتُكَ قِلادةً من حريرْ
تناسيتُ قسوةَ العيشِ المريرْ
تبقى بعيني بهيّاً كالأميرْ

*****

أنتَ يا وطني الأمّ لي فخرْ
أنتَ في وجداني ليومِ الحشَرْ
صلاتي أن يزولَ عنك الخطرْ
وأن تعودَ كما كنتَ أغرْ

*****

87

Request:
Leave Me Be

إلتماس: إتركوني

I am a Christian in Mesopotamia, my ancestors' abode.
Catholic, with all due respect to other religions in the World.
Chaldean, from progenitors to my grandchildren.
It is the loyalty that makes me proud of what is written.

Leave me be! I know when my birth is dated.
Where I lived? Is my country being decorated?
How I grew up? Which roots did my ancestors germinate?
In spite of that knowledge, I am still wanted.
Leave me be.

*****

Leave my worries, choices, tears, and laughter be.
I have my eyes, mind, ears, and measure.
I lived a past seeding my dream with weeping water.
I need to light a flame that will last forever.
Leave me be.

*****

I wear what I like in a stylish body.
I do not care if it is cheap or costly,
And whether it's been made by aloof or friendly people.
The dress is worn whether it's antique or trendy.
Leave me be.

*****

إتركوني فأنا أعرفُ تاريخَ ميلادي
أين كنت وفي أيّ البقاعِ تزهو بلادي
كيف نشأتُ ومن أيّ جذرٍ نما أجدادي
وبالرغمِ مما ترومون أعلمُ اقتيادي
إتركوني

*****

إتركوأ همّي وضحكي وخياراتي ودمعي
أنا لي عيني وعقلي وقياساتي وسمعي
عشتُ ماضٍ أبذرُ الحلمَ وأسقيه بدمعي
كمْ يدومُ اللهبُ كي أحصدَ من بعدهِ زرعي؟
إتركوني

*****

أنا ألبسُ ما يحلو لي من الشكُلِ الأنيقِ
لا أبالي السعرَ رخيصاً أومثقالَ عقيقِ
وحتى الصُنعَ غريباً أمْ من بلدٍ شقيقِ
هوَ اللبسُ باللبّاسِ لا بالعصْري والعتيقِ
إتركوني

*****

93

I was given a name on my birthday.
I grew up on a religion that showed me the way.
I am from the cradle of civilization, so proud.
Chaldeans,[34] Assyrians,[35] all have echoed loud.
Leave me be.

*****

I am a Christian in Mesopotamia,[36] my ancestors' abode.
Catholic, with all due respect to other religions in the World.
Chaldean, from progenitors to my grandchildren.
It is the loyalty that makes me proud of what is written.
Leave me be.

*****

You are free to worship God or idols or be atheist.
Worship whatever, but let the creatures be protected.
Do not kill innocent bodies in the name of God,
For all who take up the sword will perish by the sword.[37]
Leave me be.

*****

وجدتُ نفسي بعدَ الولادةِ أحملُ إسْما
نشأتُ على دينٍ خطَّ لي في الحياةِ رسْما
أفاخرُ أنني من مهدِ الحضاراتِ جسْما
كلدانيّةٌ[34], أشوريّةٌ[35], كلُّ لها في الحياةِ طعْما
إتركوني

*****

أنا مسيحيٌّ, بين النهرينِ[36] مثوى أجدادي
كاثوليكيٌّ, مع جُلِّ احترامي لأضدادي
كلدانيٌّ عن جدٍّ وأبٍ لي إلى أحفادي
هو الوفاءُ مَنْ يزهو بالحاضرِ والآبادِ
إتركوني

*****

أنتَ حرٌّ في عبادةِ اللهِ أو ألأوثانِ
أُعْبُدْ ما شئتَ ودع الخلائقَ في أمانِ
لا تقتل الجسدَ البريءَ بداع الإيمانِ
فكلُّ من يأتي بالسيفِ هوَ بالسيفِ فانِ[37]
إتركوني

*****

95

Oh' justice, among people, I see contradiction.
Atheism is becoming the scholars' obligation.
Many who opposed it yesterday are proud of it today.
Shall I follow who openly trades off the faith's way?
Leave me be.

*****

What was said in physics about God is not true.
Everyone knows that fact of the day can be myth tomorrow.
How many scientists were praised out of the blue?
Are licking, after the new discoveries, their sorrow.
Leave me be.

*****

My question: does fighting between people have reasoning?
A human since the beginning of creation is creative.
The civilization of Mesopotamia,[38] Sindh,[39] and Egypt is indicative.
Maya,[40] China, Greek, and Persian,[41] all brightening.
Leave me be.

*****

أيها العدلُ بين الأنامِ أرى تناقضا
أصبح الإلحادُ عند أهلِ العلمِ فرائضا
يزهو به منْ كان بالأمسِ لهُ معارضا
فهلْ أتبعُ منْ بالإيمانِ جهراً مُقايضا؟
إتركوني

*****

ليسَ ما قيلَ في الفيزياءِ عن الله صحيحُ
والكلُّ يعلمُ أنَّ العلمَ للعلمِ يزيحُ
فكمْ عالمٍ طالَهُ لِما اكتشفَ المديحُ؟
وجديدُ العلمِ بعدهُ بِما قالَ يُطيحُ
إتركوني

*****

تساؤلي: هل للقتالِ بين الناسِ أخلاقُ؟
هوَ الإنسانُ مذْ بدءِ الخلْقِ فكرهُ خلَّاقُ
حضارةُ النهرينِ [38] والسندِ [39] ومصرَ إشراقُ
والمايا [40] والصينَ واليونانَ والفرسِ [41] آفاقُ
إتركوني

*****

So also Roman, Aztek,[42] and Inca[43] civilization:
Each reflects its wave of light to the present generation.
Despite what is narrated from the act of extermination,
There remains a beacon who once was the smartest nation.
Leave me be.

*****

My friend, why is extremism in values and ideas?
Who said others are listless and you are conscious?
Both of you are the fabric of educative scholar,
That descends whatever and raises whoever higher.
Leave me be.

*****

I do not accept any opinion fighting human thoughts.
Every opinion can be right or wrong at some points.
Perfection is only for the one who invented the world.
What a beautiful way to present the view in sensible word.
Leave me be.

*****

كذا حضارةُ الرومانِ والأزْتك[42] والإنكا[43]
كلٌّ يلوحُ من طيِّها نورٌ ما زال يذْكى
رغمَ ما يُرْوى من فعْلِ الإبادةِ وما يُحْكى
تظلُّ نِبراساً لشعبٍ كان يوماً هو الاذكى
.إتركوني

*****

صاحِ, لِمَ التطرُّفُ في الأفكارِ والقيَمِ؟
مَنْ قالَ أنَّكَ واعٍ وغيرُكَ كالنوِّمِ؟
كلاكما مِنْ نسيجِ عالِمٍ مُتعلِّمِ
يُنزِلُ مَنْ يشاءُ أو يعلو بهِ للقِممِ
إتركوني

*****

أنا لا أرضى برأيٍ يحاربُ فكرَ البشرْ
كلُّ رأيٍ لهُ في الخطأِ والصوابِ أثرْ
فليسَ الكمالُ إلّا لِمَنْ للعالمِ ابتكرْ
ما أحلى أن يكونَ الخيرُ لكلِّ فكرٍ وطرْ
إتركوني

*****

Every single person must have ethnic roots.
Generations come and go, the ark reboots.
History has not written about a nation vanished in full.
Every nation has grown to him, throughout time, ovule.
Leave me be.

*****

Do not blame me for my affiliation and origin.
All trees of the world have a branching column.
Everyone is proud of what is open or hidden.
A human is scaled as to the values of heaven.
Leave me be.

*****

The attraction to life forgets me what happened:
Exhaustion of work left me shredded.
My body approached the death chair.
How do I survive if I am drowned in despair?
Leave me be.

*****

كلُّ فردٍ بين الأنامِ حتماً لهُ جذورُ
جيلٌ يَفْنى وجيلٌ يحيا والفلكُ يدورُ
لمْ يكتب التاريخُ عن شعبٍ لفتْهُ القبورُ
كلُّ شعبٍ نمتْ لهُ عبْرَ الزمانِ بذورُ
إتركوني

*****

عنْ انتمائي وأصلي وفصلي لا تلوموني
فأشجارُ الدُنا لها العديدُ مِنَ الغصونِ
وكلُّ امرءٍ يزخرُ بالمكشوفِ والمكنونِ
مقياسُهُ بما يحملُ مِنْ خُلُقٍ مَصونِ
إتركوني

*****

حُبُّ الحياةِ ينسيني اليومَ وما في الأمسِ
عرقُ الجبينِ زماناً أنهكَ كلَّ نفسي
ومِنْ طَعَنِ السنينِ اقتربَ الجسمُ من رمسي
كيفَ النجاةُ وأنا غارقٌ في بحرِ يأسي؟
إتركوني

*****

Oh' friend, do not accuse nations with infidelity.
Every nation is like kindergarten in diversity.
Since creation, views have never been without battles.
They were not spared throughout the time from shackles.
Leave me be.

*****

I look for lost sheep in the valley and plains.
I proclaim as to the Lord's command and ordain.
I do not care about the critics' mention and action.
Christianity was grown up by persecution.
Leave me be.

*****

يا صاحبي لا تتهم الشعوب بالإلحادِ
كلُّ شعبٍ كالروضةِ في تنوّع الأورادِ
لمْ يكُ الفكرُ منذُ الخليقةِ بلا أضدادِ
ولمْ ينجُ الرأيُ عبر الزمانِ من الأصفادِ
إتركوني

*****

أبحثُ عن خرافٍ ضالّةٍ في السهلِ والوادي
أبشّرُ بما أوصاني به ربُّ العبادِ
لا أبالي بما يقولُهُ مجمعُ النقّادِ
هيَ المسيحيةُ ترعرتْ بالإضطهاد
إتركوني

*****

Puzzlement:
Where Do I Go?

حيرة: أينَ أمضي؟

I can not tolerate a scene of food in the garbage.
Millions of hungry people suffering from self-damage.
Will the Angel of the Lord accept bribes in the Latter Day?
So the rich will find, to the Kingdom of Heaven, his way.

Is it true that God is the creator of the universe?
And whatever tragedies are happening to people, he will observe?
Is it really wisdom that all die for the Lord?
The killed or the killer, both follow his word.
Where do I go?

*****

Dispersion in every religion, heresy in every sect.
One worships God for the sake of gain.
Another adores doctrine regarded by atheism correct.
Who is the one with whom I should remain?
Where do I go?

*****

Some of the chapters in the Old Testament calls for wonder.
Legends of Babylon are, before the Torah, in order.
The story of the flood signified God's anger.
The puzzle of each symbol is determined by elders.
Where do I go?

*****

أصحيحٌ ما يُقالُ خلقَ الكونَ إلاهُ؟
وما يحصلُ للأنسِ مِنْ مآسٍ سيراهُ؟
هلْ حكمةُ الربِّ حقاً أن يفنى الكلُّ فداهُ؟
قاتلٌ أو مقتولٌ كلاهما يسعى رضاهُ
أين أمضي؟

*****

فرقةٌ في كلِّ دينٍ بدعةٌ في كلِّ مذهبْ
واحدٌ يعبدُ رباً لهُ في أمرِهِ مأربْ
آخرٌ يعشقُ فكراً هوَ للإلحادِ أقربْ
يا تُرى مِنْ ذا الذي إليهِ أنقادُ وأذهب
أين أمضي؟

*****

بعضُ ما في العهدِ القديمِ يدعو إلى العَجَبِ
أساطيرُ بابلَ قبلَ التوراةِ بالنَسَبِ
قصةُ الطوفانِ نذيرُ اللهِ بالغَضَبِ
رموزٌ يُحَددُ لُغْزَها اجتهادُ المَذْهَبِ
أين أمضي؟

*****

109

The first crime since creation was Cain killing Abel.[44]
From the adultery of Abraham[45] with a slave came Ishmael.[46]
Because of David's[47] lust, a husband was, to the war, thrown.
How many damsels got a crown from Solomon?[48]
Where do I go?

*****

After all those sins, they are, in the Bible, prophets.
How can a revelation equalize sinners with innocents?
Will the drunkenness of Noah[49] be like the Baptist's[50] piety?
Or the chastity of a Saint as the whim of laity?
Where do I go?

*****

One third of the world suffers from hunger.
Another third is oppressed by a tyrant ruler.
The last third enjoys prosperous living.
People will doubt the justice of the Lord of being.
Where do I go?

*****

ألقتْلُ مذْ بدءِ الخليقةِ أصلُهُ قابيلُ[44]

ومِنْ زِنى ابراهيمَ[45] بالعبْدَةِ أتى اسماعيلُ[46]

وزوجٌ مِنْ شهوَةِ داودَ[47] بالحربِ قتيلُ

وكمْ حسناءً عليها مِنْ سليمانَ[48] إكليلُ؟

أين أمضي؟

*****

وبعدَ تِلْكَ المعاصي هُمْ بالكتابِ أنبياءْ

كيفَ للوحْي أنْ يساوي الخطاةَّ بالأنقياءْ؟

فهلْ تقوى المعْمداني[49] كسُكْرِ نوحَ[50] بالعراءْ؟

أمْ عِفّةُ القديسينَ كنَزَواتِ الحكماءْ؟

أين أمضي؟

*****

أين أمضي وثلثُ العالمِ من الجوعِ يشكو

وثلثٌ لهُ من الحاكمينَ ظلمٌ وهتكُ

وثالثُ منهما يتنعمُ هوَ المُلْكُ

كيفَ يا ربَّ العبادِ بعدلِكَ لا يُشَكُّ؟

أين أمضي؟

*****

111

It is the will of God that the creators are different.
Many whose brains are charged with science may be insolvent.
But more ignorants are, in harvesting money, competent.
Does the contradiction suggest the cosmos is by the Lord dwelt?
Where do I go?

*****

The wisdom of the Almighty is to those who believe in his power.
Thanks to him, despite the impact of tragedy and horror,
The family of the victims hallow his greatness.
The instinct of self is: loving the worship of holiness.
Where do I go?

*****

Who seduced Eve is named in the Bible as serpent.
Left as a devil, different people met.
Proclaiming the virtues, same as curate.
Many might think that he is a saint.
Where do I go?

*****

إرادةُ اللهِ هذي وفي خلْقِهِ شؤونُ
يحيا فقيراً مِنْ دماغُهُ بالعلمِ مشحونُ
ويحصدُ مالاً مِنْ عقلُهُ بالجهلِ مسجونُ
هل التناقضُ يوحي الكونَ بالربِ مسكونُ؟
أين أمضي؟.

*****

حكمةُ الباري لمِنْ آمنَ بهِ من الناسِ
حمْداً لهُ رغمَ هوْلِ المصائبِ والمآسي
أهلُ الضحايا باسمهِ تُسَبّحُ وتواسي
غريزةُ النفسِ أن تهوى عبادةَ الأقداسِ
أين أمضي؟

*****

مِنْ أغوى حواءَ أسموهُ بالكتابِ إبليسا
غادر الأرضَ وعاد بين الأنامِ جليسا
يزهو بوعظِ الفضيلةِ تخاله قسّيسا
ربما يُطوّبُ يوماً فيدعوه قدّيسا
أين أمضي؟

*****

113

The demons of earth are in every spot.
Misguided thought and treachery to them is a comfort.
Preaching the word of God, many accept their dirt.
Whoever asks to leave them, he will be called apostate.
Where do I go?

*****

The conflicts are going beyond barriers.
No genuine solutions by the super powers.
Who foresees incentive encouragement from ego lovers?
Even the preacher of faith is a winner of pleasures.
Where do I go?

*****

The way of life is paved with contradiction.
Many who cry about the faith have falsehood intention.
Careless about Commandments, facing the logic with rejection.
Either silence or frankness with high valuation.
Where do I go?

*****

أين أمضي وشياطينُ الأرضِ في كلِّ بقعهْ؟
ضَلالُ الفكرِ والغدرِ عندهم مصدرُ المتعهْ
كلامُ الله يتلوهُ وقومٌ يرضى بالخدعهْ
فمنْ نادى اتركوهمْ, قالوا من ذا صاحبُ البدعهْ
أين أمضي؟

*****

أين أمضي والصراعاتُ تتعدى الحواجزْ؟
كلُّ منْ على السلطةِ بالحلولِ لها عاجزْ
منْ يرتجي من عاشقِ الأنا تشجيعَ الحوافزْ؟
حتى واعظُ الإيمانِ باللذات هو فائزْ
أينَ أمضي؟

*****

أين أمضي وطريق الحياةِ فيه تناقضْ؟
يبكي على الإيمانِ منْ دنياهُ صارتْ فرائضْ
لا يبالي بالوصايا هو للمنطقِ رافضْ
فإما السكوتَّ أو للصراحةِ سعرٌ باهضْ
أين أمضي؟

*****

115

Whenever I read history, I drown in deep sorrow.
Christianity of yesterday is not as today or tomorrow.
The Apostles proclaimed the power of God for salvation without limit,
And baptized in the name of the Father, Son, and Holy Spirit.
Where do I go?

*****

Render to Caesar: what is Caesar's, and to God what is God's.[51]
Love the Lord your God, follow Jesus's words.
Why are God's commandments forgotten by most?
The shepherds without the Gospel are therefore lost.
Where do I go?

*****

The Church across time was separated into churches.
From the new churches emerged many branches.
These small branches are in desperate debate.
Whoever is present there tries to dictate.
Where do I go?

*****

كلما أطالعُ التاريخَ أغرقُ بالحزنِ
هيَ المسيحيةُ بدءً كانت كما في ذهني
رسلٌ طافتْ ببشرى الخلاصِ في كلِّ ركنِ
وعمدتْ بالروحِ القدسِ والآبِ وبالإبنِ
أين أمضي؟

*****

ما للهِ لله وما لقيصرَ لقيصرْ[51]
أعطوا كما المسيحُ في أورشليمَ بها أمرْ
فلمَ كلماتُ ربي تغدو لكانَ خبرْ؟
لو الرعاةُ بغيرِ الأناجيلِ لا تؤتمرْ
أين أمضي؟

*****

كنيسةٌ عبرَ الزمانِ انشقتْ عنها كنائسْ
ومنْ تلكَ الكنائسِ صارت اليوم مجالسْ
وما يجري في هذي المجالسِ نقاشٌ يائسْ
ما دام الحاضرُ على حريرِ السلطةِ جالسْ
أين أمضي؟

*****

How many scientists were burned by the prelacy?
How many diligent theologians were accused of heresy?
Whoever sought to reform was excommunicated by the boss.
Everyone who disagreed faced what is worse.
Where do I go?

*****

A pastor leaves today and tomorrow, comes alternative.
People of the church are in dispute, with whom to be positive?
Some laugh joyfully, others are left in tears.
The loyalty to their village takes away their fears.
Where do I go?

*****

The ailment of churches is not finding a cure.
The hitch is a mafia having, in each term, a tactical brochure.
The treatment is obeying the priest's request.
Prescription is affected by conflict of interest.
Where do I go?

*****

زماناً كم عالمٍ باسم الصليبِ أحرقوهُ؟
وكم مجتهدٍ باللاهوتِ عِلماً هرطقوهُ؟
ومنْ سعى لإصلاحِ الكنيسةِ حرموهُ
وكلَّ منْ خالف الرأيَ يومها عزلوهُ
أين أمضي؟

*****

أليوم راعٍ راحلٌ وغداً آتٍ بديلُ
وجمعُ الكنيسةِ في صراعٍ لِمَنْ يميلُ
بعضٌ يضحكُ فرَحاً ودمعُ البعضِ يسيلُ
ولاءُ القريةِ طاغٍ على الإيمانِ دخيلُ
أين أمضي؟

*****

عجَباً لداءِ الكنائسِ لا يلقى شفاءا
فالعلّةُ مافياتٌ في كلِّ عهدٍ لها باعا
علاجها ما يأمرُ به الكاهنُ يُطاعا
ولكنَّ البلْسَمَ في المصالحِ لا يُراعى
أين أمضي؟

*****

119

Why does the priest think of the sin as infallible?
Is he the substitute of the Lord for everything capable?
Or it is the vanity and ego circling his word?
Is he really deprived from the delights of the world?
Where do I go?

*****

Some of the churches at night look like nightclubs.
The bulletin board carries singers, dancers, and drabs.
The shepherd spots the dollar shining.
Yes, Bernard Shaw,[52] everybody search for what is missing.
Where do I go?

*****

Others have holiday hymns.
Protestants, Orthodox, or Latins.
Woe to churches stuffed with deceits.
To vicars glorifying themselves through building fleets.
Where do I go?

*****

لِمَ الكاهنُ يظنُّ عن الخطإِ معصومٌ؟
هلْ هوَ بديلُ الربِّ بالعالمينَ مهمومٌ؟
أم أنَّ الغرورَ وهوى الأنا بها محكومٌ؟
أحقاً يا تُرى مِنْ مباهجِ الدنيا محرومٌ؟
أين أمضي؟

*****

بعضٌ منَ الكنائس في الليلِ غدتْ مراقصْ
لوحةُ الإعلاناتِ فيها مطرباتٌ وراقصْ
وراعٍ من خلالها يبصرُ الدولارَ شاخصْ
نعمْ برنّاردشو[52] كلُّ يبحثُ عن ما فيه ناقصْ
أين أمضي؟

*****

وأخرى في كلِّ عيدٍ لها حفلُ التراتيلِ
لاتينيةٌ كانت أم من أتباعِ الأناجيلِ
أسفي على كنائسي تُحشى بالأباطيلِ
يبغي رعاتُها جاهاً من بناءِ الأساطيلِ
أين أمضي؟

*****

But among them, some stuck to their vows,
The choir chanting in the mass, the church glows.
No clamor, no belly dancing, no tipsiness.
And no excuse of acquaintance tempting someone else.
Where do I go?

*****

In every era, Christianity was troubled with contest.
Adoring the positions, the faith being left.
The Redeemer's call for unity, when was it obeyed?
In the Day of Resurrection, no excuse or defense will aid.
Where do I go?

*****

Why has Christianity experienced schisms?
How many churches in the East have become wrecks?
What about the cohorts of the cross forced to be Muslims?
And the procession of the martyrs with martyrs met.
Where do I go?

*****

لكنْ بينهم على النذور باقٍ كما قبلا
جوقةُ الترانيم تشدو بالقداسِ ما أحلى
لا صخبٌ ولا هزُّ الخصرِ وهْيَ بالخمرِ ثملى
ولا حجةُ التعارفِ تُغري من لهُ أصلا
أين أمضي؟

*****

في كلِّ عهدٍ لنا بالمسيحيةِ صراعُ
هيَ المناصب من عشقها الإيمانُ يُباعُ
نداءُ المخلّصِ للوحدةِ متى يُطاعُ؟
فهلْ يُجدي يومَ القيامةِ عُذرٌ أو دفاعُ؟
أين أمضي؟

*****

لمَ المسيحيةُ من أمسٍ تعاني انقساما؟
وكمْ من الكنائسِ في الشرقِ صارت حطاما؟
وماذا عن أفواجِ الصليبِ أُجبرتْ إسلاما؟
ومواكبُ الشهداءِ بالأجسادِ تُداما
أين أمضي؟

*****

123

Died on the cross, thrown to the lions' ground.
Never denied the faith, became more admired.
Alas, the patrons are not interested anymore.
Filling their pockets, that is what they adore.
Where do I go?

*****

How do long daydreams supersede the facts?
The conviction is people will not get their rights.
The rights are in a deep coma, and never wake up.
The justice is hanged like a dark lamp.
Where do I go?

*****

Heresy, knock, knock! Jesus is at the door.
Jehovah's Witnesses[53] desecrate the Bible's core,
Claiming the Redeemer is a prophet, nothing more.
Denying the Trinity, the Lord's gospel, they ignore.
Where do I go?

*****

على الصليبِ ماتتْ للإسودِ سيقتْ طعاما

لم تنكرُ الإيمانَّ بل زادَ عشقاً وهياما

غابَ ما كان قديماً ليس للراعي اهتماما

غيرَ أن يملأ جيباً بالحلالِ أو حراما

أين أمضي؟

*****

إلى متى أحلامُ اليقظةِ تسري في العروقِ؟

والقناعةُ أنَّ الشعبَ لن يحضى بالحقوقِ

فالحقُّ عمْقُ سباته غيبوبةُ المصعوقِ

والعدلُ حلَّقَ عالياً بربطةِ المشنوقِ

أين أمضي؟

*****

هرطقةٌ أطرقْ أطرقْ فعندَ البابِ يسوعُ

شهودُ يهوه[53] تفتري هيَ للحقِّ شموعُ

تحسبُ الفاديَ أنساً عنهُ يشتطُّ الخشوعُ

تنكرُ الثالوثَ رباً إنجيلَهُ لا تُطيعُ

أين أمضي؟

*****

125

Mormons[54] created polygamous godly mates.
Revelation revealed verses written on golden plates.
Jesus left Jerusalem to America with hands scarred.
How does an intellect follow an illusional mind?
Where do I go?

*****

What kind of religion appeals to celebrities to follow?
The ladder is climbed by whoever is, to the curriculum, thorough.
The blasphemy emerged from science fiction.[55]
The writer tempted for a fallacy mission.
Where do I go?

*****

Ask justice, why is sedition from the same zone?
Is it really a coincidence or a strategy of Zion?[56]
Split the church, a plan put forward long time ago.
Apostatize from the origin, driven by human ego.
Where do I go?

*****

جعلَ المورمونُ[54] مِنَ الخالقِ مِزواجاً وأبْ
أنزلَ الوحيَ كتاباتٍ على ألواحٍ ذَهَبْ
غادرَ القدْسَ لأمريكا وفي كفَّيْهِ نُدَبْ
عجباً للعاقلِ أن يتبع رؤيا من كذَبْ
أين أمضي؟

*****

أيُّ دينٍ يستهوي من المشاهيرِ أتْباعا؟
يصعدُ السُّلَّمَ مِنْ للمنهجِ مِمضي ابتياعا
بزغثْ أركانُهُ مِنْ قصةٍ لاقت سماعا
أصبحَ الكاتبُ للطامحِ معبوداً مُطاعا[55]
أين أمضي؟

*****

أسألُ العدلَ لِمَ الفتنةُ مِنْ نفسِ المكانِ؟
هلْ هيَ الصدفةُ حقاً أم من تدبيرِ ساسانٍ[56]؟
زيدوا الكنائسَ قيلتْ حقبةً قبل الزمانِ
يرتد عن الأصل طوعاً من ليسَ بالحسبانِ
أين أمضي؟

*****

127

Today, I am a guest in life; I will travel tomorrow.
I do not know which is the way, and who to follow.
I am convinced that whoever is on earth will inevitably depart.
Bodies on top of bodies are in the graves quiet.
Where do I go?

*****

Who does good will cast abundant good.
Who sows evil shall harvest bitter food.
The train of life is heading towards the same destiny.
A gnashing of teeth is the fate or joyful harmony.
Where do I go?

*****

To think I undermined my faith is misapprehension.
Are the most critical of the church theological people?
How many lovers suffer from their loving passion?
Yes Gandhi,[56] the problem is not with Christianity but Christian.
Where do I go?

*****

أنا اليوم ضيفٌ على الحياةِ غداً مسافرْ

لا أدري كيف السبيلُ ومَنْ مِنْ قبلي يهاجرْ؟

كلُّ علمي مَنْ على الأرضِ حتماً بعدي يغادرْ

هيَ الأجسادُ على الأجسادِ نامتْ بالمقابرْ

أين أمضي؟

*****

مَنْ يصنعُ الخيرَ يلقى في الخلدِ خيراً وفيرا

ومنْ يزرعُ الشرَّ حصاده نبتاً مريرا

قطارُ العمرِ ماضٍ نحو منْ رسمَ المصيرا

فرحُ هناك أو الأسنان تشكو صريرا

أين أمضي؟

*****

مَنْ يظنُّ أني عن الإيمانِ زاغٍ واهمُ

كمْ ناقدٍ للكنيسةِ باللاهوتِ فاهمُ؟

وكمْ حبيبٍ يعاني وهْوَ بالعُشْقِ هائمُ؟

وما قالهُ غاندي [57] في الواقعِ حقاً قائمُ؟

أين أمضي؟

*****

129

I am with faith despite being a medical doctor.
I am with science; the faith frames my skillful picture.
The design of the universe is the work of a Creator.
Moronic is the one who is not aware of Christian culture.
Where do I go?

*****

Whenever I distance myself from faith, I feel ashamed.
Whenever I hear the name of Christ, I bow my head.
Those who prostrate, are by His grace saved.
Jesus is my love, my salvation, in my soul is based.
Where do I go?

*****

Alas, Churches are like the Mafia; each party is double-faced.
Each clings on a piece of bun planning to engulf the whole bread.
The ambition of the ego demands in the name of Christianity.
The voice of truth rises alone and fights for liberty.
Where do I go?

*****

أنا مع الإيمانِ رغمَ ما أملكُ من عِلْمٍ

أنا معَ العِلْم وإيماني يُزيدُ مِنْ فهمي

تصميمُ الكونِ إبداعُ الخَلْقِ بالشَّكْلِ والجسمِ

بصيرٌ مَنْ لا يعي مصابٌ بالصُّمِّ والبُكْمِ

أين أمضي؟

*****

كلما اقتربتُ منَ الإيمانِ نسيتُ بؤسي

أينما سمعتُ إسمَ المسيحِ أحنيتُ رأسي

يسجدُ الشعبُ لمَنْ لأجلهِ مشى لرمسٍ

هوَ حُبّي وخلاصي كيف لا أفديه نفسي

أين أمضي؟

*****

ألكنائسُ مافياتٌ والأحزابُ مناصبُ

كلٌّ على قطعةٍ من الكعكِ يتكالبُ

طموحُ الأنا باسمِ المسيحيةِ يُطالِبُ

وصوتُ الحقِّ لوحدهِ يعلو ويُحارَبُ

أين أمضي؟

*****

131

I can not tolerate a scene of food in the garbage.
Millions of hungry people suffering from self-damage.
Will the Angel of the Lord accept bribes in the Latter Day?
So the rich will find, to the Kingdom of Heaven, his way.
Where do I go?

*****

What I see in the same scene makes me vomit.
Some of the past darknesses, today, are lit.
Others are drowned in actions lacking dignity.
All are behind the director in the theatre of absurdity.
Where do I go?

*****

I will walk on every trail leading to the truth.
I do not care about the length of the track for reaching my booth.
The testimony of the right is my aim, no matter the insult.
From the school of life, I learned when to react.
Where do I go?

*****

أنا لا أستسيغُ مشهدَ أكلٍ في القمامهْ
والملايينُ مِنَ الجياعِ أضحتْ كالحُطامهْ
هلْ يرضى ملاكُ الربِّ رشوةً يومَ القيامهْ؟
كيْ يدخلَ الغنيُّ الملكوتَ رافعَ الهامهْ
أين أمضي؟

*****

ما أرى في نفس المشهدِ يدعو إلى القَرَفِ
بعضُ من متحفِ القديمِ يجْتَرُّ وا أَسَفي
وبعضٌ تاهٍ لا يعي الصحيحَ منَ الخَرَفِ
والكلُّ وراءَ المُخرج في مسرح السَخَفِ
أين أمضي؟

*****

أنا سالكٌ كلَّ دربٍ للحقيقةِ يُفْضي
لا أبالي طولَ المسارِ وكمْ به سأقضي
مقولةُ الحقِّ همّي مهما جابهتُ من بُغْضِ
فمنْ مدرسةِ الحياةِ علمتُ أين أمضي
أين أمضي؟

*****

133

My Heart Story:
Who Is To Help?

قصةُ قلبي: فمَنْ يُعينْ؟

Tarik Mikhael
2019

Oh' Creator, to you my love, loyalty, and my praise.
When I remember my survival, my faith will rise.
All the knowledge I own is a gift from God.
How could I pay back who kept me around?

Oh' my heart, why you do not soften?
You disturb my silence every now and then
As you take me to heaven.
By aspirin,[58] life is written to me again.
Who is to help?

*****

Do not trust your heart in two faces:
When falling into the trap of love affairs,
And when the blood in the arteries is scarce.
A human will harvest agony in both cases.
Who is to help?

*****

The torment of love despite the bitterness tastes sweet.
Whoever drowned in devotion is mired with hankering.
The heart hiccup will be echoing: welcome to choking.
After each passion the hug is intensified with heat.
Who is to help?

*****

أيُّها القلبُ الراقدُ في صدري لِمَ لا تلينْ؟
تُعَكِّرُ صفاءَ سُكوني بين حينٍ وحينْ
كأنَّكَ تبتغي اقتيادي لِمثوى الراقدين
لكنَّ الحياةَ تُكتَبُ لي بفِعْلِ الأسبرينْ[58]
فمِنْ يُعينْ؟

*****

لا تأمَنْ فؤادَكَ في وجهينِ, أوَّلُهُما
حينما يسقطُ في شراكِ الحُبِّ مُسْتسلِما
وثانٍ, حين يبخلُ الشريانُ عليه دَما
هوَ الإنسانُ مِنْ كِليْهِما يحصُدُ الألَما
فمِنْ يُعينْ؟

*****

عذابُ العُشْقِ رغمَ المرارةِ حلْوُ المذاقِ
فكلُّ غريقٍ في الهوى يغوصُ باشتياقِ
ومِنْ شهقةِ القلبِ صدىً أهلاً بالإختناقِ
وبعدَ كلِّ لوعةٍ يشتدُّ حِمى العناقِ
فمِنْ يُعينْ؟

*****

139

How can I forget you, my heart, you are the pulse of my soul.
These arteries have let you down four times.
You stayed adamant despite the horror of the fall.
You were the best for postponing the time of my demise.
Who is to help?

*****

In Baghdad, two decades ago, I suffered a heart attack
Among a group of elite doctors in the right medical track,
Speaking about organ transplantation that I chaired.
Between a collection of mercy my body was laid.
Who is to help?

*****

Two arteries of my heart were sclerosed,
Both branching from the left. The right has a story:
Three stents[59] were implanted, giving my life a reward.
I stayed for a decade without sigh or worry.
Who is to help?

*****

كيفَ أنساكَ يا قلبي وأنتَ نبضُ حياتي؟
خذَلتْكَ الشرايينُ أربعاً من المرّاتِ
وأبيتَ أنْ لا تصمدَ رغمَ هولِ الوقْعاتِ
فكنتَ خيرَ مَنْ يؤجّلُ لي وقتَ مماتي
فمِنْ يُعينْ؟

*****

قبلَ عقْديْنِ فيكِ بغدادُ انتابني الألْمُ
بين نُخْبَةٍ من الاطباءِ تتكلّمُ
في ندوةِ غرْسِ الأعضاءِ أنا أتحكّمُ
ومع جمْعِ الرحمةِ عن علّتي أُتمِتُمُ
فمِنْ يُعينْ؟

*****

كان لي من الشبكاتِ[59] في شريانينِ حِصّهْ
كلاهما نبعُ الأيسرِ, وللأيمنِ قِصّهْ
ثلاثٌ لُصقتْ بالجدارِ, للحياةِ فرصهْ
صرتُ أكثرَ من عِقْدٍ بلا ألمٍ أو غصّهْ
فمِنْ يُعينْ؟

*****

141

Oh' England, from you is my science and training.
In between your folds, I forgot my sickness,
As if I was young lad exercising,
Climbing the hills up and down without weariness.
Who is to help?

*****

But you, Canada, I came to you compelled.
My path got dark, though it was bright.
You hit three main arteries of my heart.
Ten stents in the left and right dwelled.
Who is to help?

*****

I will not question the will of the Lord.
Death or life can be His word.
Every living creature will vanish later:
A plant or animal or human character.
Who is to help?

*****

بلادُ الإنكليزِ ومنكِ تدريبي وعلمي
نسيتُ بين ثناياكِ ما عانيتُ من سَقْمِ
كأني في ريْعانِ الشبابِ أُلاعِبُ جسمي
أجوبُ الطريقَ صعوداً نزولاً بلا سأمِ
فمِنْ يُعينْ؟

*****

أمّا أنتِ يا كندا فجِئْتُكِ مُسَيَّرا
وجدتُ طريقي أظْلماً كان قبلاً نيّرا
أصبْتِ شرايينَ قلبي أمِناً وأيسرا
غَدَتِ الثلاثُ شبكاتٍ اليومَ عَشْرا
فمِنْ يُعينْ؟

*****

مشيئةُ الربِّ سَلباً أو إيجاباً لا أجادِلْ
وحكمُ الخالقِ موتاً أو حياةً له ماثِلْ
كلُّ حيٍّ على كوكبِ الارضِ بالغدِ زائِلْ
نباتٌ كانَ أمْ حيوانٌ أو إنسانُنا العاقِلْ
فمِنْ يُعينْ؟

*****

Oh' Creator, to you my love, loyalty, and my praise.
When I remember my survival, my faith will rise.
All the knowledge I own is a gift from God.
How could I pay back who kept me around?
Who is to help?

*****

I will not stop praying and supplication.
I will keep repeating "Our Father in Heaven"[60]
With "Hail Mary"[61], asking her for intercession.
I will follow the Sermon of the Mount's[62] lesson.
Who is to help?

*****

I will never forget who quenched the flame of my anguish,
And planted in my heart the seeds of the best wish.
Thanks to God who maintained the freshness of the flowers
And kept my wife and the kids away from sad matters.
Who is to help?

*****

لكَ يا خالقي حبّي ووفائي وامتناني

متى ما ذكرْتُ نجاتي يستزيدُ إيماني

كلُّ ما أملكُ مِنْ عِلْمٍ أنت الذي أعطاني

كيفَ أردُّ الجميلَ لِمَنْ بالعيْشِ أبقاني؟

فمِنْ يُعينْ؟

*****

أنا لنْ أكُفَّ عن الدُعاءِ والصلواتِ

سأصلّي دوماً أبانا الذي في السمواتِ[60]

وأتلو السلامَّ عليكِ[61] يا أسمى القدّيساتِ

وأسجُدُ لعِظَةِ المسيحِ في التطويباتِ[62]

فمِنْ يُعينْ؟

*****

لا لن أنسى مَنْ أخمدَ في فؤادي لَظى الأنينْ

ومَنْ غرسَ في جنانِ الدارِ بذورَ الحنينْ

رَبِّي الذي أدامَ النُضْرَةَ في زهْرِةِ الياسْمينْ

وأبعدَ الزوجةَ والأكبادَ عنْ يومٍ حزينْ

فمِنْ يُعينْ؟

*****

145

Footnotes

ألهوامش

1. Mary: Virgin Mary, mother of the Lord Jesus Christ.
2. Caesar: Julius Caesar was a Roman general and politician who named himself dictator of the Roman Empire, a rule that lasted less than one year.
3. Thomas the Apostle: one of the Twelve Apostles of Jesus according to the New Testament.
4. Motherland: referring to Iraq.
5. Mosul: a major city in northern Iraq.
6. Tel Kaif: a Chaldean town in Nineveh Governorate, northern Iraq.
7. Baghdeda : a Syriac town in northern Iraq.
8. Tikrit: a city in Iraq.
9. Telleskuf: a Chaldean town in northern Iraq.
10. Bakufa: a Chaldean district in northern Iraq.
11. Alqosh: a Chaldean district located in northern Iraq.
12. Dohuk : a city in northern Iraq.
13. Tigris and Euphrates: The Tigris is the eastern of the two great rivers that define Mesopotamia, the other being the Euphrates.
14. Cradle of Civilization: Mesopotamia, the area between the Tigris and Euphrates rivers (in modern day Iraq), is often referred to as the cradle of civilization because it is the first place where complex urban centers grew.
15. Babylon: the most famous city from ancient Mesopotamia whose ruins lie in modern-day Iraq 59 miles southwest of Baghdad.
16. Persians: an ethnic group from the country of Iran. They are the direct descendents of ancient Indo-Iranians (Aryans),
17. Sumer: is the earliest known civilization in the historical region of southern Mesopotamia, modern-day southern Iraq.
18. Babylon: was a key kingdom in ancient Mesopotamia from the 18th to 6th centuries BC.
19. Assyria: was a Mesopotamian kingdom and empire of the ancient Near East, perhaps as early as the 25th century BC until its collapse between 612 BC and 609 BC.

1. ألعذراء: إشارة إلى مريم العذراء أم يسوع المسيح.

2. قيصر: إشارة إلى يوليوس قيصر الذي أعلن نفسه دكتاتوراً لروما, ودام حكمه بعد ذلك أقل من عام.

3. توما الرسول: أحد تلاميذ المسيح الإثني عشرة حسب العهد الجديد.

4. ألبلد الغالي: إشارة إلى العراق.

5. ألموصل: من أكبر مدن شمال العراق.

6. تلكيف: قضاء ضمن محافظة الموصل في شمال العراق.

7. بغديدا: مدينة سريانية ضمن محافظة الموصل شمال العراق.

8. تكريت: محاظة في وسط العراق.

9. تلسقف: ناحية كلدانية ضمن محافظة الموصل شمال العراق.

10. باقوفة: ناحية كلدانية ضمن محافظة الموصل شمال العراق.

11. ألقوش: ناحية كلدانية ضمن محافظة الموصل شمال العراق تحوي ضريح النبي ناحوم.

12. دهوك: محافظة ضمن كردستان العراق.

13. دجلة والفرات: أكبر نهرين في العراق من إلتقائهما في الجنوب يتكون شط العرب.

14. مهد الحضارات: إشارة إلى حضارة وادي الرافدين (ألعراق حالياً).

15. بابل: من أقدم مدن وادي الرافدين, وتبعد آثارها 59 ميلاً عن بغداد عاصمة العراق.

16. ألفرس: مجموعة إثنية من إيران الحالية ومن أصل آري.

17. سومر: مهد أول حضارة في التاريخ نشأت في الجزء الجنوبي من العراق الحالي.

18. بابل: مفتاح ممالك وادي الرافدين بين القرن 6-18 قبل الميلاد.

19. آشور: مملكة وإمبراطورية امتدت من شمال العراق إلى الشرق الأدنى منذ القرن 25 قبل الميلاد لحين سقوطها بين عام 612 و 609 قبل الميلاد.

20. Mongol: empire founded by Genghis Khan in 1206. Conquered nearly all of continental Asia, the Middle East and parts of Eastern Europe.
21. ISIS: Islamic State of Iraq and Syria.
22. Marrakesh: a major city of the Kingdom of Morocco.
23. Damascus: the capital of the Syrian Arab Republic.
24. Baghdad: the capital of Iraq and has a long and illustrious history.
25. Hulagu: was a Mongol conqueror who sacked Baghdad in 1258.
26. Jihadi or Jihadist: refers to a person who believes that an Islamic state governing the entire community of Muslims must be created.
27. al-Baghdadi: Abū Bakr al-Baghdadi is the leader of the Islamic State of Iraq and Syria (ISIS) militant terrorist organization.
28. "All who draw the sword will die by the sword": derived from the Gospel of Matthew (Matthew 26, 26:52).
29. "Revelation of John": the apocalyptic text forming the final book of the New Testament.
30. Sunni: the largest denomination of Islam. Its name comes from the word Sunnah, referring to the behavior of the Islamic prophet Muhammad.
31. Shiites: the second largest branch of Islam, originated as a political movement supporting Ali (cousin and son-in-law of Muhammad, the Prophet of Islam) as the rightful leader of the Islamic state.
32. Dhimmi: a historical term referring to non-Muslim subjects of a Muslim state.
33. Quran: the Islamic sacred book written down in Arabic.
34. Chaldeans: an ancient people group who inhabited what would today be southern Iraq.
35. Assyrians: people who have lived in the Middle East since ancient times.
36. Mesopotamia: an ancient region between the Tigris and Euphrates rivers, now Iraq.
37. For all who take up the sword will perish by the sword: a proverb derived from the Gospel of Matthew (Matthew 26, 26:52).

20. ألمغول: إشارة إلى إمبراطورية المغول التي أسسها القائد جنكيزخان عام 1206 وغزت معظم آسيا والشرق الأوسط وجزء من اوربا الشرقية.

21. داعش: مختصر ألدولة الإسلامية في العراق والشام.

22. دمشق: عاصمة الجمهورية السورية.

23. مراكش.: مدينة مهمة في المغرب العربي.

24. بغداد: عاصمة جمهورية العراق ولها تاريخ مميّز.

25. هولاكو: قائد مغولي حقق غزو بغداد عام 1258 وأسقط الخلافة العباسية.

26. المجاهد أو الجهادي: إشارة الى كل من يؤمن بخلق دول إسلامية تحكم باسم القران والسنة.

27. ألبغدادي: نسبة إلى أبو بكر البغدادي مؤسس الدولة الإسلامية في العراق وسوريا وقائد تنظيم داعش.

28. 28. كل من جاء بسيف به يقتل: قول المسيح بحسب إنجيل متى (26: 52).

29. رؤيا يوحنا: آخر فصل في العهد الجديد يصور مصير العالم بإشارات رمزية.

30. ألسني: من أتباع أكبر المذاهب الإسلامية, والإسم مشتق من كلمة « السنّة » في إشارة إلى سلوك نبي الإسلام محمد.

31. ألشيعي: من أتباع ثاني أكبر المذاهب الإسلامية التي نشأت كحركة مؤيدة للإمام علي إبن عم النبي محمد وزوج إبنته.

32. ذمّي: تسمية قرآنية لغير المسلم الساكن في الدولة الإسلامية ولا بد أن يدفع الجزية ثمناً لحياته.

33. ألقرآن: ألكتاب المقدس للمسلمين وكتب باللغة العربية أولاً.

34. ألكلدان: من سكان العراق الأصليين الذي سكنوا قديماً جنوب العراق الحالي.

35. ألآشوريون: من سكان العراق الأصليين الذين أخضعوا دولاً كثيرة لسيطرة أمبراطوريتهم.

36. بين النهرين: ألمنطقة بين نهري دجلة والفرات والمعروفة تاريخياً بموسوبوتاميا والتي تشمل جزءً من العراق الحالي.

37. فكلُّ من يأتي بالسيفِ هوَ بالسيفِ فاني: مقتبس من قول المسيح حسب البشير متي (26, 26 – 52).

38. Mesopotamian civilization:first in the world 3500BC-500BC. Current location in Iraq.
39. Sindh or The Indus Valley civilization: 3300 BC-1900 BC. Current locations: Afghanistan, Pakistan, India.
40. Mayan civilization: 2600 BC-900 BC. Current locations: Mexico, Guatemala, Belize, El Salvador, and Honduras.
41. Persian civilization: 550 BC–331 BC. Current location Modern-day Iran.
42. Aztek civilization: 1345 AD-1521AD. Current location Mexico.
43. Incan civilization: 1438 AD-1532 AD. Current location Ecuador, Peru, and Chile.
44. 44.Cain and Abel: the first two sons of Adam and Eve according to the biblical Book of Genesis.
45. Abraham: the first of the Hebrew patriarchs and an important fulfillment of God's promise.
46. Ishmael: Abraham's son, born to Hagar.
47. David: the second king in the ancient Israel.
48. Solomon: one of King David's three sons.
49. Noah: built Noah's ark before the Flood.
50. Baptist: referring to John the Baptist.
51. Render to Caesar what is Caesar's, and to God what is God's: Matthew 22:21.
52. Bernard Shaw: an Irish playwright, critic, polemicist and political activist.
53. Jehovah's Witnesses: a millenarian restorationist Christian denomination with non trinitarian beliefs distinct from mainstream Christianity.
54. Mormons: most often refers to members of The Church of Jesus Christ of Latter-day Saints (LDS Church) because of their belief in the Book of Mormon.
55. Scientology: is a body of religious beliefs and practices launched in May 1952 by American author L. Ron Hubbard (1911–86).
56. Zion: is a place name often used as a synonym for Jerusalem as well as for the biblical Land of Israel as a whole.

38. حضارة النهرين: بين دجلة والفرات 3500 – 500 قبل الميلاد . ألعراق حالياً.

39. حضارة السند: بين 3300 – 1900 قبل الميلاد . ألهند, باكستان, وأفغانستان حالياً.

40. حضارة المايا: بين 2600-900 قبل الميلاد . ألمكسيك, غواتيمالا, بليز, ألسلفادور, وهندوراس حالياً.

41. ألحضارة الفارسية: بين 550 – 331 قبل الميلاد. إيران حالياً.

42. حضارة الأزتك: بين 1345 – 1521 بعد الميلاد. ألمكسيك حالياً.

43. حضارة الإنكا: بين 1438 -1532 بعد الميلاد. الإكوادور, بيرو, وشيلي حالياً.

44. قايين وقابيل: أولاد آدم وحواء حسب سفر التكوين في العهد القديم.

45. إبراهيم: أول أنبياء اليهود الذي التزم بوعد الرب.

46. إسماعيل: إبن إبراهيم من العبدة هاجر.

47. داود: ألملك الثاني لمملكة إسرائيل القديمة.

48. سليمان: أحد أبناء داود الثلاثة.

49. ألمعمدان: إشارة إلى يوحنا المعمدان.

50. نوح: أتم بناء السفينة المعروفة بإسمه قبل الطوفان.

51. ما لله لله وما لقيصر لقيصر: مقتبسة من قول المسيح بحسب البشير متى (22:21).

52. برنادشو: كاتب مسرحي آيرلندي الأصل, ناقد ساخر وناشط سياسي.

53. شهود يهوه: طائفة مسيحية ترميمية لا تؤمن بالثالوث المقدس وتختلف بالإيمان عن المسيحية السائدة.

54. ألمورمون: غالباً ما تشير إلى أعضاء كنيسة المسيح لقديسي اليوم الأخير بسبب إيمانهم بكتاب المورمون.

55. الساينتولوجي: مجموعة من المعتقدات والممارسات الدينية التي أطلقها الكاتب الأمريكي ل. رون هوبارد (1911-1986) في مايو 1952

56. صهيون: هو اسم مكان يستخدم غالبًا كمرادف للقدس وكذلك لأرض إسرائيل التوراتية ككل.

57. Gandhi: an Indian activist who was the leader of the Indian independence movement against British colonial rule.
58. Aspirin: medication commonly used as a pain reliever and to reduce fever. It is also an anti-inflammatory drug and can be used as a blood thinner.
59. Stent: A tube designed to be inserted into a vessel or passageway to keep it open.
60. "Our Father in Heaven": the Lord's prayer.
61. Hail Mary: (Latin: Ave Maria) is a traditional Catholic prayer asking for the intercession of the Blessed Virgin Mary, the mother of Jesus.
62. Sermon of the Mount: is Jesus' longest speech and teaching in the New Testament, and occupies chapters 5, 6 and 7 of the Gospel of Matthew.

57. غاندي: ناشط هندي كان زعيم حركة الاستقلال الهندية ضد الحكم الاستعماري البريطاني. سبق وأن قال «مشكلتي ليست مع المسيحية بل مع المسيحيين».

58. الأسبرين: دواء يستخدم عادة كمسكن للألم وللحد من الحمى كما أنه دواء مضاد للالتهابات ويمكن استخدامه لزيادة سيولة الدم.

59. الشبكات: إشارة إلى الدعامات المصممة كإنابيب تلصق بجدران الأوعية الدموية لإبقائها مفتوحة.

60. أبانا الذي في السموات: الصلاة الربانية التي علمها المسيح لتلاميذه لتلاوتها كصلاة.

61. السلام عليك يا مريم: (لاتينية: أفا ماريا) هي صلاة كاثوليكية تقليدية تطلب شفاعة السيدة العذراء مريم والدة يسوع.

62. عظة الجبل: هو أطول خطاب تعليمي ليسوع في العهد الجديد، ويحتل الفصول 5 و 6 و 7 من إنجيل متى.

About the Author

Sabah Michael Yacoub was born in Iraq from a Chaldean family. He descended from the native inhabitants who entered Christianity in the era of St.Thomas the Apostle, one of the Twelve disciples of Jesus Christ.

He graduated from Baghdad Medical School and received a higher degree from the United Kingdom. He spent years of his life practicing his specialty of internal medicine and cardiology.

He moved from Baghdad to the United Kingdom after the Allied invasion of Iraq. Then he migrated to North America, traveling between Canada and the United States.

Despite his scientific background, he has a deep inclination toward knowledge culture in general and toward poetry in particular. He started writing poetry during high school, but left his beautiful hobby only to return back to it recently.

Sabah was inspired by the tragic circumstances that have afflicted his motherland and by the injustice, displacement, and abuse of Christians, Sabians, and Yazidis minorities, as expressed in the two poetry quartets *Tragedy: How Often and How Much?* currently in print, and *Flashes of the Present Pain*, that is in your hands now.

Additionally, Sabah writes on various topics in his mother tongue on ankawa.com, alqosh.net, and some magazines and newspapers produced in the diaspora.

His main interests are watching sports, especially soccer, and participating in various cultural and educational activities. He also loves collecting used books, especially religious and historical ones.

Sabah is married with two daughters and one son.

His wisdom in life "What matters is not your achievement, but to be creative in what you have achieved».

"It is a blessing gifted by God to anyone who grows a charming flower from a bud planted in a field not of his specialty".

He can be reached at his email: sabahyacoub2013@gmail.com.

نبذة عن الكاتب

ولد في العراق من عائلة كلدانية تنحدر جذورها من سكان البلا د الاصليين الذين دخلوا المسيحية على يد القديس توما الرسول احد التلاميذ الإثني عشر للفادي يسوع المسيح.

تخرج من كلية طب بغداد, ونال الشهادة العليا من المملكة المتحدة, وقد أمضى سنين حياته في ممارسة أختصاصه بالأمراض الباطنية والقلبية.

إنتقل من بغداد إلى المملكة المتحدة بعد اجتياح الحلفاء لأرض العراق, ومنها هاجر إلى أمريكا الشمالية متنقلاً بين كندا والولايات المتحدة الأمريكية.

بالرغم من خلفيته العلمية إلا أنه يمتلك ميلاً عميقاً للثقافة المعرفية عموماً وللشعر خصوصاً. وسبق أن بدأ محاولات متعددة في نظم الشعر في المرحلة الثانوية ثم ترك هوايته الجميلة لفترة من الزمن عاد إليها في السنوات الأخيرة, حيث ألهمته الظروف المأساوية التي حلّت على وطنه الام وما حصل من تعسف وتشريد وتنكيل, ولا يزال, بحق الأقليات الإثنية من المسيحيين والصابئة المندائيين والإيزيديين, وقد عبّر عنها جزئياً في الرباعيتين الشعريتين الموسومتين « تراجيديا: كم مرة كم؟ » التي هي تحت الطبع حالياً, و» ومضات الألم الحاضر» التي في يد القارئ الكريم الآن.

كما انه كاتب يكتب في مواضيع متنوعة بلغته الام في موقعي عنكاوة.كوم وألقوش.نت, وأيضاً في بعض المجلات والصحف الصادرة في بلاد المهجر.

يهوى متابعة البطولات الرياضية وخاصة كرة القدم, والمساهمة في النشاطات الثقافية المتنوعة, كما انه يعشق شراء وجمع الكتب المستعملة وبالأخص الدينية والتاريخية منها.

متزوج وله إبنتان وولد واحد

حكمته في الحياة « ليس المهم من أنت ومن تكون, بل أن تُبدع في ما أنت عليه وستكون.» «إنها لنعمة وبركة يغمر الخالقُ بها كلَّ من أينعت له زهرة يافعة من برعم غرسه في حقل ليس من إختصاصه.»

بالإمكان الإتصال بريده الألكتروني:
sabahyacoub2013@gmail.com

157

Human grievances are multiple and complex, yet it is better to live oppressed than unjust. The physical and psychological wounds may continue with the continuation of those grievances, but there is still a glimmer of hope that frames the present pain gradually. The image then turns to look like a ray from the sun enveloping the oppressed with warmth and light in the hope that the page of injustice will be folded forever and be part of the painful past.

With the burden of injustice, the oppressed shall speak to Virgin Mary Mother of Jesus, crying out, *Where are you?*

From the severity of suffering, they will search for another savior to complain to.

And with the continuation of injustice, they will shout eagerly, *Whom do I call?*

When the oppressed sees the disintegration and decaying of the wounded motherland, they will ask, *Who is to blame?*

Nevertheless, they will pray and call for the secular system as a way of salvation.

From the depth of desperation and the extent of despair, they will beg and say, *Leave me be.*

Despite the needs, the suffering, the appeals, the questioning, the wishes and dreams, they will be puzzled by the obscure fate and wonder where to go.

This modest book tells in the first seven quartets the story of the present pain that envelops the body of those suffering from the pitfalls of life and the injustice of others.

It is concluded by the last quartet that strengthens my faith in the Almighty Creator who saved me from repeated heart attacks and kept me breathing between my friends and my beloved.

نص غلاف الكتاب

مظالم الإنسان متعددة ومتشعبة, ورغم ذلك فالأفضل أن يعيش المرء مظلوماً لا ظالماً. قد يستمر الجرح الجسدي والنفسي مع استمرار تلك المظالم ولكن تظل هنالك ومضة من الأمل تؤطر بشعائها لوحة الألم الحاضر تدريجياً فتبدو الصورة بعدئذ كشعاع شمس يلف المظلوم بالدفء والنور على أمل أن تطوى صفحة الظلم إلى الأبد وتصبح ضمن الماضي الأليم.

فمع وطأة الظلم يناجي المظلوم أمه العذراء صارخاً أين أنت ؟

ومن شدة معاناته يبحث عن منقذ آخر له يشتكي.

ومع استمرار الظلم يصيح بصوت عالٍ من أنادي؟

وحينما ينظر الى بلده الام الجريح وما آل إليه من خراب ودمار يسأل من يلاما ؟

ورغم ذلك يتغنى به ويدعو إلى النظام العلماني كطريق للخلاص.

ومن عمق يأسه ومدى قنوطه يتوسل قائلاً إتركوني.

ورغم مناجاته ومعاناته ومناداته وتساؤلاته وتوسلاته وأمنياته

يشعر بالحيرة من أمره مستفسراً أين أمضي؟

وشاءت الأقدار أن تداهمه النوبة القلبية مرة بعد مرة, وفي كل نوبة يحاط برعاية الرب الكريم متجاوزاً الحدث الجسدي الاليم ليهمس شاكراً رحمته: فمن يعين؟

يحكي هذا الكتاب المتواضع في سبع رباعيات قصة الألم الحاضر الذي يغلف جسد المتألم من مآزق الحياة وظلم أخيه الإنسان. ثم يختتمها بالرباعية الأخيرة التي تعزز إيمانه بالخالق القدير لإنقاذه من عاتيات الزمن كما أنقذ قلبه من نوباته الحادة والمتكررة.